CW01500582

LEADING DIGITAL CHANGE: A PRACTICAL GUIDE FOR PRODUCT OWNERS, PMS, AND INNOVATION LEADERS

Proven Frameworks to Deliver AI-Powered Solutions, Accelerate Transformation, and Build Winning Teams

SIMONE SALVO

Independently published

Innovation distinguishes between a leader and a follower.
Steve Jobs

About the Author

I'm Simone Salvo, and I've spent the last decade helping companies navigate digital transformation—not just with frameworks and tools, but with real conversations, tough decisions, and the occasional existential crisis over a product backlog.

My journey started somewhere between lines of code and business models. With a background in computer science and economics, I quickly found myself fascinated by the space where technology meets people—and where innovation becomes messy, political, and wonderfully human.

I've worked across fintech, AI, cloud platforms, and enterprise software, leading teams, building roadmaps, and asking annoying questions like "But what problem are we *really* solving?" I've managed products in highly regulated industries, led Agile transformations, and coached teams through uncertainty and change.

Writing is how I make sense of all this. My previous books explored how individuals and nations alike can rethink their future through technology. With *Leading Digital Change*, I wanted to create something more grounded—a practical guide for those in the trenches of change: product owners, PMs, innovators, and anyone trying to move the needle without losing their sanity.

When I'm not mapping out digital strategies or facilitating yet another retro, you'll find me cycling, scribbling ideas in messy notebooks, or diving into books about systems, psychology, and why everything is more connected than we think.

This book is the result of experience, curiosity, and countless conversations with people like you. I hope it helps. And if it doesn't, at least I promise it won't waste your time.

in linkedin.com/in/simonesalvo

Preface

When I first started working in technology, I thought that knowing how things worked was enough. If you could master the code, the architecture, the tools—then surely success would follow.

I was wrong.

Over time, I began to see that the biggest blockers to progress weren't technical—they were human. Misalignment, fear of change, lack of clarity, broken communication, conflicting incentives. These were the real bottlenecks. The hard part wasn't building a feature—it was getting people to agree on *why* we were building it in the first place.

And that's when I realized: leading digital change is not a technical problem. It's a leadership one.

This book was born out of that realization. Not from a sudden insight, but from a decade of trial, error, late nights, stakeholder battles, MVP launches, transformation initiatives that almost broke me—and others that made me fall in love with this work all over again.

I've had the privilege of working in different industries,

from banking to SaaS, from cloud-native startups to complex enterprises bound by regulation and legacy. I've worn many hats: developer, product owner, scrum master, strategist, team coach. And across all of these roles, one thing has stayed consistent—change is hard, but it's also the only way forward.

We talk a lot about disruption, innovation, agility. But behind every buzzword is a team of real people trying to make things better. This book is for them.

It's for the product owner trying to balance vision and delivery.

For the project manager tasked with making sense of chaos.

For the tech lead who sees the future clearly but struggles to get buy-in.

For the executive who wants transformation but isn't sure where to begin.

And for anyone who wakes up in the morning knowing that what worked yesterday might not work tomorrow.

This isn't a book of theory. It's not a manifesto. It's a field guide.

I won't give you a "magic framework" that solves everything. Instead, I'll offer you practical tools, real stories, and hard-earned lessons—things I wish someone had told me earlier in my career. Each chapter is designed to be actionable. You can read it end to end, or you can jump straight to the part you need today.

We'll explore how to lead when no one gave you permission to. How to align people around outcomes instead of outputs. How to make AI useful instead of just impressive. How to ship value incrementally without losing the big picture. And how to survive (and maybe even enjoy) the messy middle of change.

One thing I've learned is this: successful transformation

doesn't start with technology. It starts with people. With conversations. With trust. With the courage to ask "What if?"—and the resilience to keep going when the answer is complicated.

Change is never just digital. It's emotional, political, cultural. It affects identity and power and process. If you want to lead it, you need more than Jira tickets and KPIs —you need empathy, clarity, and the willingness to challenge what's comfortable.

In these pages, I've tried to capture not just what to do, but how it feels to do it. Because leading digital change isn't just a role—it's a mindset. One that combines ambition with humility, direction with adaptability, and urgency with patience.

So whether you're a leader by title or by attitude, whether you're just starting out or deep in the trenches, I hope this book helps you feel a little more equipped—and a little less alone.

Because the future won't wait.

And the change you're hoping for? It starts with you.

To the quiet leaders.
The ones who drive change not with noise, but with intention.
Who build trust before processes, and listen before they speak.
Who question the status quo—not to complain, but to improve.
Who believe that technology should serve people, not replace them.
To everyone who's ever asked "Why are we doing this?"
and stayed in the room long enough to help find the answer.

This is for you.

Contents

Foreword   xv

Part I

Why Change Fails

Understanding the Invisible Forces Blocking Progress

The Illusion of Control   5
The Culture Clash   20
Speed vs. Alignment   36

Part II

Building the Foundation for Change

Tools, Mindsets, and Conversations That Make
Change Possible

Leading from the Middle   55
From Output to Outcome   70
Designing for Real Humans   85

Part III

Making Change Real

How to Execute with Purpose and Ship What Matters

The Art of Prioritization   103
Working Across Silos   118
Feedback Loops That Work   133

Part IV

Sustaining the Momentum

From Launch to Legacy: Keeping Change Alive

Change as a Habit   157
Leading Through Uncertainty   172
Becoming a Change Catalyst   191

Bibliography   209

Foreword

I didn't set out to write a book on leading digital change. What I set out to do was survive it.

Over the years, I've been at the center of projects that promised transformation but delivered confusion. I've been in rooms where buzzwords flew faster than decisions, and where "agility" meant working weekends. I've witnessed the excitement of bold visions collapse under the weight of unclear goals, poor communication, or outdated mindsets. And I've also seen transformation work—seen teams come alive, products launch with purpose, and cultures evolve for the better.

Somewhere along the way, I began collecting patterns. I noticed what made change stick—and what made it stall. I watched how the best leaders didn't just drive digital initiatives; they created clarity, built trust, and empowered people to act. And I realized that while technology may be the enabler, the real work of transformation is deeply human.

This book comes from that experience.

It's not a manual. It's not a heroic tale. It's a field guide, written by someone who's been deep in the trenches of change—as a product owner, a scrum master, a strategist, and above all, as someone who cares deeply about building things that matter.

If you're holding this book, chances are you're one of the people trying to lead from the middle: not at the top, not always on the front lines, but somewhere in between—connecting, translating, aligning. Maybe you manage products. Maybe you lead teams. Maybe you're the person everyone looks to when things get messy. Or maybe you're just the one asking the uncomfortable questions. Wherever you are, this book is for you.

It's for those of us who know that transformation isn't just about technology. It's about priorities. Culture. Incentives. Fear. Hope. Timing. And it's about learning how to lead when no one hands you the playbook.

You'll find practical tools in these pages—things you can apply on Monday morning. You'll also find stories and reflections, moments that might sound a lot like your own. I've included what worked for me, what didn't, and what I'm still trying to figure out. Because leading change isn't about having all the answers. It's about learning in public. Iterating. And showing up consistently even when things are unclear.

I wrote this book to remind myself—and maybe you too—that we're not here to implement processes. We're here to create impact. We're not here to serve systems. We're here to serve people. And we're not here to chase transformation for its own sake—we're here to shape a future that's more intelligent, more human, and more aligned with the values we care about.

You won't find dogma in these chapters. You'll find questions. You'll find uncomfortable truths. And hopefully, you'll find clarity, or at least a little more language for the conversations we need to have.

Because digital change is everywhere. The real question is: who will lead it with purpose?

If this book helps you move one conversation forward, lead one meeting better, or navigate one tough decision with more intention—then it has done its job.

And if it inspires you to keep showing up, to keep building, and to keep believing in the value of thoughtful leadership in a noisy world—then I couldn't ask for more.

Thank you for reading. Let's get to work.

PART I
Why Change Fails

UNDERSTANDING THE INVISIBLE FORCES
BLOCKING PROGRESS

There's a strange irony in the world of digital transformation: everyone agrees that change is necessary, yet very few understand why it so often fails. The buzz around innovation, agility, and disruption is louder than ever, and still, the majority of transformation programs either stall, implode, or fade into irrelevance. Why?

The first answer people reach for is technology. Wrong tools. Legacy systems. Technical debt. While those are real obstacles, they're rarely the root cause. In my experience, the real reasons are far more elusive—and far more human.

This first part of the book is dedicated to exploring exactly that: the invisible forces that quietly sabotage our best intentions. Forces like fear, misalignment, organizational inertia, misplaced urgency, and cultural resistance. These are not things you'll find in a roadmap or Gantt chart, yet they shape every transformation effort from the inside out.

I've sat in countless project kick-offs where excitement filled the air, budgets were approved, timelines were defined, and leadership nodded in unison. And I've watched as, weeks or months later, the same initiative turned into a political battlefield, or quietly bled to death through scope creep, competing priorities, and the slow erosion of trust. It doesn't happen because people are lazy or incompetent. It happens because organizations are complex systems—and complex systems resist change by default.

Change touches everything. It rewires incentives, challenges identities, forces decisions, and invites scrutiny. And most people—whether consciously or not—don't want to change. They want to improve, yes. But improve without disrupting what they know. Without letting go of control. Without confronting the possibility that their current way of working may be part of the problem.

This part of the book is about facing those truths without sugarcoating them.

We begin with the illusion of control—how our desire to manage uncertainty often leads us to over-plan, over-promise, and ultimately under-deliver. In environments dominated by complexity, control becomes a comforting myth. It allows us to feel safe while walking straight into chaos.

Then we move into the cultural dimension. Culture is what people do when no one is watching. It's how meetings are run, how decisions are made, how dissent is treated, and how failure is processed. And it plays a massive, often invisible role in determining whether change will be nurtured or strangled. A team can have all the right tools and still be paralyzed by unspoken fears or outdated norms.

We'll also confront the dangerous trade-off between

speed and alignment. In the rush to "go digital," many organizations sacrifice clarity for movement. They ship faster, but with less purpose. They pivot, but without direction. They confuse motion with progress—and eventually lose the confidence of the very people they're trying to lead.

My goal here is not to criticize, but to illuminate. To give voice to the obstacles no one wants to name. To explore why smart people with good intentions still struggle to drive meaningful change. Because if we can't understand why change fails, we'll keep repeating the same patterns—more tools, more frameworks, more dashboards —but with the same disappointing results.

What follows in the next three chapters is not a diagnosis. It's an exploration. A walk through the hidden dynamics that sabotage transformation before it even begins. These aren't academic theories; they're based on conversations, hard lessons, and real-world experience from the messy middle of change.

Understanding why change fails is not a pessimistic exercise—it's the first act of leadership. Because once we see clearly, we can act differently. We can stop blaming tools and start building trust. We can stop chasing perfection and start creating momentum. We can stop waiting for certainty and start leading through complexity.

This part of the book invites you to pause. To observe. To challenge your assumptions. To look beneath the surface of stalled initiatives and ask the harder question: what's really in the way?

Let's find out.

The Illusion of Control

WHY GOOD PLANS FAIL AND HOW TO FACE
COMPLEXITY

PLANS, CONTROL, AND COMFORT
How we confuse structure with certainty

We love plans. We love their neatness, their predictability, the illusion they create that the future can be shaped like a spreadsheet. A well-organized roadmap, a Gantt chart with perfectly aligned dependencies, a backlog prioritized down to decimal points—these artifacts give us the feeling that we are in control. They signal progress, professionalism, and foresight. But in the world of digital transformation, that sense of control is more often a sedative than a strategy.

Most transformation efforts begin with a plan that feels solid. There's a kickoff, a timeline, a vision statement. Budgets are allocated, teams are formed, goals are defined. On paper, everything makes sense. But within weeks, the real world shows up. Dependencies shift. Stakeholders change their minds. Technical constraints emerge. Legal blocks something unexpected. A vendor fails to deliver. Or worse, the users behave nothing like we assumed they would.

This is where the illusion reveals itself: the idea that we can "control" change in a complex environment is comforting—but false. The more uncertainty we face, the more we tend to retreat into structure. We plan harder, document more, tighten the process. But in doing so, we're often avoiding the truth: that no amount of planning can fully anticipate what's coming.

This doesn't mean planning is useless. Far from it. Planning is essential—but its value is in the process, not the plan itself. It's in the alignment it creates, the conversations it sparks, the assumptions it surfaces. A good plan is not a map—it's a compass. It doesn't tell you exactly where to go, but it helps you navigate when the landscape shifts.

The danger comes when we mistake plans for reality. When we fall in love with our timelines and milestones to the point where we ignore the signals around us. We say things like "but the plan says Q3" while everything around us screams "this isn't working." We defend deadlines instead of asking better questions. We perform predictability for stakeholders, instead of embracing the real complexity of the work.

Why do we do this? Because control feels safe. It protects us from chaos. It allows us to look competent. It reassures our stakeholders, our teams, and—most of all—ourselves. Control is part of our professional identity. To admit that we can't predict everything feels like a failure. But it isn't. It's reality. And the most effective leaders I've worked with are not the ones who hold on tightest to their plans. They're the ones who know when to adapt.

Facing complexity means being honest about what we don't know. It means planning in shorter cycles, listening more, and measuring what matters. It means designing systems that can absorb change instead of collapsing under it. It means trading rigidity for responsiveness, and certainty for clarity.

We have to stop treating digital transformation like a linear project. It's not a building you construct; it's a living system you evolve. And like any living system, it's dynamic, unpredictable, and often surprising. The goal is not to eliminate that unpredictability—it's to work with it.

In many ways, the desire for control is deeply human. But in the context of transformation, it can be a trap. The more we try to lock things down, the less adaptive we become. The more detailed our blueprints, the more fragile our execution. Real change requires resilience, not rigidity.

So the next time you feel tempted to anchor yourself in a perfect plan, ask yourself: what am I really trying to control? And what might happen if I let go—just a little?

Because in the end, it's not control that makes us strong. It's our ability to move forward even when things don't go according to plan. And that begins with seeing the illusion for what it is.

THE SEDUCTION OF CERTAINTY
Why we mistake predictability for progress

There's a particular kind of comfort that comes from believing we know what's going to happen. It's not just a professional instinct—it's a psychological need. In uncertain environments, the promise of predictability becomes seductive. We convince ourselves that with enough planning, enough metrics, enough meetings, we can create stability. We can anticipate every risk, preempt every deviation, and engineer success. But what if that certainty is only an illusion we create to soothe ourselves?

In complex systems, predictability is not a feature—it's a false promise. Digital transformation efforts are rarely linear. They involve shifting goals, emerging constraints, evolving technologies, and most of all, human behavior that refuses to be scripted. And yet, despite all this, we continue to cling to the idea that we can forecast and control outcomes as if we were dealing with fixed inputs in a closed environment.

The corporate world has institutionalized this desire for certainty. We build business cases that require assumptions to become facts. We present timelines as guarantees rather than hypotheses. We talk about delivery in quarters and cost savings in percentages, as if the world will stand still long enough for our models to prove accurate. The reality, of course, is very different. Markets shift. Leadership changes. Priorities evolve. New constraints appear. And what looked certain six weeks ago becomes irrelevant today.

The danger isn't just that we're wrong. It's that we base critical decisions on being right. We structure teams, allocate budgets, and manage expectations around plans that assume stability. And when reality doesn't comply, we don't revisit the model—we blame the execution. We call it poor performance or a lack of commitment, when in truth, the problem was our insistence on predictability in an unpredictable environment.

This isn't to say that planning or structure has no value. But when predictability becomes the goal, we stop learning. We become less curious, less flexible, less willing to experiment. We optimize for efficiency instead of adaptability. And that's when transformation begins to rot from the inside. It becomes performance theatre—everyone doing what they're supposed to, reporting progress, meeting deadlines, but no one actually challenging whether what's being delivered still matters.

One of the greatest shifts in mindset that leaders must make is moving from "How do I make this certain?" to "How do I navigate this uncertainty with clarity?" Because clarity and certainty are not the same. Certainty is rigid; clarity is responsive. Certainty tells you what will happen; clarity helps you understand what's happening. One locks you into a path; the other helps you adjust as the path unfolds.

Clarity allows for movement. It invites continuous feedback. It accepts that the plan might change, not because of failure, but because of learning. It requires the humility to admit what we don't know, and the courage to act anyway. In many ways, clarity is harder than certainty—because it forces us to stay present. To listen, question, and respond in real time, rather than hide behind a predefined trajectory.

Organizations that thrive in change don't pretend to know the future. They invest in sensing it. They create space for course correction. They build systems that prioritize learning over perfection, and culture that values adaptability over compliance. These are not easy things to measure, and they don't look as polished in a PowerPoint deck. But they are the foundation of real, sustainable progress.

The need for certainty is understandable. It makes us feel safe. It helps us explain our decisions. It keeps the anxiety at bay. But if we let it guide us, it will quietly drain the life out of our most ambitious efforts.

Progress doesn't come from certainty. It comes from movement, from discovery, from being willing to act without full visibility. If we can accept that, we can begin to lead in a way that is not only more honest—but far more powerful.

THE CONTROL PARADOX
How trying to control complexity makes it worse

There's an old truth in systems thinking: the more tightly you try to control a complex system, the more likely it is to resist you. It's a paradox that many leaders experience but few acknowledge. In the world of digital transformation, this paradox shows up everywhere—in overengineered governance, in micromanaged teams, in inflexible roadmaps that collapse at the first sign of change. The harder we grip the system, the more chaotic it becomes.

We often assume that more control leads to better outcomes. If only we define more processes, hold more meetings, centralize more decisions, then surely the results will improve. But what actually happens is the opposite. Teams slow down. Creativity fades. Decision-making bottlenecks. Fear creeps in. People stop experimenting and start protecting themselves. The system becomes less responsive, not more.

This is the control paradox in action: our attempts to reduce complexity end up amplifying it. What begins as a desire for structure becomes an architecture of rigidity. Instead of enabling change, we begin managing exceptions to a plan that no longer fits the reality we're in. And before long, transformation becomes a negotiation between conflicting controls, each pulling in a different direction.

At the heart of this paradox is a misunderstanding of what kind of system we're operating in. In complicated systems—like building a bridge or assembling a car—control can work well. Inputs are predictable, outcomes are repeatable, and expertise can guide success. But digital transformation lives in the realm of complexity, not complication. Here, cause and effect are not always clear.

Outcomes emerge through interaction. What worked last time may fail this time for reasons no one anticipated.

In complex systems, the goal isn't to eliminate unpredictability. It's to increase the system's capacity to adapt. That means loosening control in strategic ways. It means distributing decision-making to the edges, where the information is freshest. It means replacing rigid plans with guiding principles, and status reports with honest conversations. It means treating people not as executors of tasks, but as intelligent agents capable of sensing and responding to change.

Of course, this kind of leadership can feel terrifying. It demands trust. It challenges traditional hierarchies. It forces leaders to relinquish the comfort of being the one with all the answers. But it also unlocks something powerful: the collective intelligence of the system. When people are free to move, sense, and act with purpose, the system becomes not just more adaptive—but more alive.

This doesn't mean chaos. It means coherence. The difference lies in intent. In chaos, actions are disconnected and reactive. In coherence, actions are aligned but decentralized. There is a shared understanding of purpose, of values, of direction—even if the exact steps change along the way. This is what great transformation leadership creates: not control, but coherence.

One of the most powerful shifts a leader can make is from asking "How do I get people to follow the plan?" to "How do I create the conditions for success, even if the plan changes?" That shift reframes control not as a function of command, but as a function of design. You design for adaptability. You create structures that allow for movement. You measure learning, not just progress.

The irony is that when you stop trying to control everything, you often get more of what you were chasing in the first place—engagement, ownership, alignment, velocity. Not because you forced it, but because you created space for it to emerge.

Digital transformation will always carry complexity. That's not a flaw—it's the nature of the work. The question is whether we respond with fear and control, or with clarity and trust. The answer defines not just the success of your initiative, but the kind of culture you're building along the way.

Trying to control complexity is like trying to hold water in your hands. The tighter you squeeze, the more you lose. But if you learn to cup your hands just right, you can carry more than you ever thought possible.

WHEN CONTROL MEETS FEAR
The emotional roots of resistance to uncertainty

We rarely talk about emotion in digital transformation. The conversation tends to orbit around systems, metrics, frameworks, and tools—as if change were a purely technical exercise. But underneath every decision, every delay, every act of resistance, there's emotion. And often, that emotion is fear.

Fear is the quiet engine that drives much of the need for control. It rarely announces itself directly. It shows up as caution, process obsession, defensive language, or excessive documentation. It's embedded in phrases like "we can't afford to get this wrong," or "we need to manage expectations," or "let's wait until it's clearer." Fear is not always irrational; in fact, it often has good reasons. But when it's not acknowledged, it becomes a hidden force shaping behavior—and not always in helpful ways.

Fear makes us crave certainty. It makes us cling to plans because we're afraid of ambiguity. It makes us centralize decisions because we're afraid of mistakes. It makes us avoid conflict because we're afraid of misalignment. And above all, it makes us act like the future is knowable, so we can stop feeling vulnerable about not knowing.

This is where the illusion of control becomes most dangerous. It doesn't just mislead us—it protects us emotionally. It gives us something to hold onto. It lets us feel responsible without being exposed. But in doing so, it often steers us away from the real work of transformation, which requires honesty, courage, and the willingness to move forward without guarantees.

Fear also shows up in how we lead others. Leaders who are afraid—of losing face, of being challenged, of not having answers—often create environments where control is confused with stability. Teams learn to protect themselves. They stop speaking up. They stop taking risks. They start optimizing for safety instead of learning. Innovation slows, but few people notice, because everything still looks organized. The slide decks are polished. The deadlines are met. But beneath the surface, the system is stagnant.

It's important to say: fear is not weakness. It's a natural response to risk. But it becomes corrosive when we let it shape our systems in secret. The leaders I respect most are not the ones who show no fear—they're the ones who know how to name it, face it, and move through it. They create spaces where people can talk about what feels unclear or risky. They normalize uncertainty. They model curiosity instead of defensiveness. And in doing so, they make transformation possible.

This emotional honesty is rare, especially in high-stakes environments. But it's powerful. When people feel psychologically safe, they're more likely to be honest about risks, faster to share concerns, and more open to experimenting. Control becomes less about command and more about connection—about understanding where the fear lives and addressing it directly.

In one transformation I supported, the turning point wasn't a new process or tool. It was a moment in a leadership meeting when someone finally said, "I'm afraid we're pretending we have clarity when we don't." That statement shifted the entire tone of the project. Suddenly, others admitted they were confused too. A new conversation emerged—one grounded not in pretending to be certain, but in committing to discover together.

Fear doesn't disappear just because we act brave. But it stops controlling us when we bring it into the open. When we recognize that the need to control everything isn't a leadership strength—it's often a sign that something deeper needs attention.

If we want to lead meaningful change, we have to do more than manage complexity. We have to understand our own emotional relationship to it. That starts with acknowledging that fear is there, that it's human, and that it doesn't need to be fixed or hidden—it needs to be heard.

Transformation is not just about changing systems. It's about changing how we relate to uncertainty—and to ourselves. Control can't protect us from the unknown. But awareness can help us navigate it with more wisdom, more humility, and more impact.

TOWARD A NEW UNDERSTANDING OF CONTROL
Letting go without falling apart

To lead meaningful transformation, we must learn to think differently about control. Not to discard it entirely, but to reframe it—to move from the idea of control as domination toward control as design. This shift requires us to fundamentally rethink what it means to lead in uncertainty, and to accept that the kind of control we're used to—predictive, top-down, tightly managed—is no longer fit for the systems we operate in today.

Letting go of traditional control does not mean falling into chaos. It does not mean abandoning strategy, discipline, or responsibility. Quite the opposite. It means building a new kind of control—one based on trust, responsiveness, and systemic coherence. It means creating structures that allow movement without falling apart, and teams that are capable of navigating complexity without waiting for instructions.

The old model of control is built on the idea that someone, somewhere, must always be in charge—that with the right authority, the right rules, and the right reporting, outcomes can be guaranteed. But this model breaks down in environments of continuous change. It creates bottlenecks, delays, disengagement. It demands knowledge and foresight from leaders that no one can reasonably possess in such dynamic conditions.

The new model asks something different. It invites us to lead through conditions rather than commands. It invites us to shape culture rather than dictate outcomes. It pushes us to focus on principles rather than prescriptions, and to create feedback loops that allow the system to correct itself.

This kind of control is more subtle. It's less visible, and less immediately satisfying. You can't point to it in a dashboard or a weekly report. It's measured not in adherence, but in adaptability—not in how closely people follow the plan, but in how skillfully they respond when the plan changes.

And make no mistake: the plan *will* change. That's the only real constant in digital transformation. What matters is how your organization responds when it does. Do people freeze, waiting for instructions? Do they panic, blame, resist? Or do they regroup, reorient, and move forward with a shared sense of purpose?

This is where true leadership shows up. Not in having all the answers, but in creating the conditions where others can discover them. Not in predicting every risk, but in fostering the resilience to respond. Not in enforcing certainty, but in cultivating clarity and trust—even when the path is unclear.

There's a kind of maturity that comes with letting go of the illusion of control. It's a quiet confidence, built not on perfection but on presence. It says: I may not know exactly what will happen, but I know how we will respond. I know what we value. I know how we decide. I know what matters most.

This understanding reframes failure, too. Instead of something to avoid at all costs, failure becomes data. A signal. A necessary part of learning. In this model, control isn't about avoiding mistakes—it's about building systems that recover, adapt, and grow stronger because of them.

Letting go in this way doesn't make us weak. It makes us more effective. It allows us to lead change without being crushed by it. It invites us to move with the system, not against it—to recognize patterns, sense shifts, and act with agility rather than rigidity.

As we close this chapter, I invite you to reflect: Where in your work are you holding on too tightly? What would it look like to let go—not recklessly, but intentionally? What new forms of control might emerge if you trusted the system, your team, and yourself just a little more?

Because in the end, real control isn't about eliminating uncertainty. It's about being ready for it. And that readiness comes not from clinging to the old, but from building the capacity to thrive in what comes next.

The Culture Clash

COLLIDING REALITIES
Why transformation feels harder than it should

On paper, digital transformation seems straightforward. You identify inefficiencies, implement new tools, reorganize teams, and embrace agile ways of working. The vision makes sense, the roadmap is plausible, and the technology is available. Yet when you step inside the organization and start the real work, everything slows down. Meetings drag, decisions get delayed, confusion spreads, and suddenly what looked like a bold leap forward becomes a careful negotiation with the past.

This tension doesn't stem from poor planning or resistance for the sake of it. It comes from something deeper: the cultural collision between the future you're trying to build and the present you're trying to fix. Transformation requires alignment across domains that speak different languages, carry different assumptions, and often operate under conflicting incentives. When technology, business, and legacy systems converge, you're not just managing complexity—you're managing different realities.

Tech teams, for instance, often operate in a world of iteration, speed, and technical precision. Their mindset is driven by architecture, automation, and the desire to reduce friction through code. Business stakeholders, on the other hand, are grounded in risk, cost, market value, and measurable results. Their horizon is often shorter, more financial, and constrained by operational needs. Then there's legacy—both in terms of systems and mindset. These are the processes, beliefs, and structures that have been in place for years, sometimes decades, and have built their own internal logic of how things "should" work.

When these three forces meet, they don't merge—they collide. And unless the organization is aware of this collision, transformation becomes a series of misunderstandings. Technology gets built that doesn't serve real needs. Business expectations get set without understanding feasibility. Legacy processes get bypassed without addressing the political consequences. What emerges is a landscape of passive resistance, superficial alignment, and frustrated teams pointing fingers at each other.

This cultural clash is often invisible at first. It hides behind polite conversations, vague agreements, and phrases like "we're aligned in principle." But underneath, there's tension. The tech team wants to automate a workflow, but the business team still needs paper records for audit. The product owner wants to experiment, but compliance demands full documentation upfront. Leaders talk about empowerment, but decisions still get escalated up the chain.

Transformation stalls not because people aren't smart or motivated, but because they're operating in systems that reward different behaviors. Culture is not what's written on the company's website—it's what happens when pressure hits. It's how people make decisions when there's ambiguity. It's how they respond to failure, how they ask for help, how they deal with conflicting priorities.

When you introduce change, you're not just changing tools or structures. You're challenging identities. A process owner who's been doing the same thing for 15 years may see your new platform not as innovation, but as a threat. A manager who built their career on controlling information may struggle to adjust to transparent workflows. These reactions are not irrational—they're emotional, and deeply human.

Understanding this is key. Leading transformation means stepping into this cultural conflict with empathy and awareness. It means translating between worlds, creating shared language, and acknowledging what's being asked of people—not just in terms of tasks, but in terms of letting go of familiarity and control.

It also means slowing down to go faster. Taking the time to align not just on goals, but on values. To clarify not just the "what" of the transformation, but the "why." To listen for unspoken fears, legacy loyalties, and political undercurrents that might block change even when everyone says yes in the meeting.

Culture clashes don't resolve themselves with new software or agile ceremonies. They require leadership. The kind that doesn't shy away from the discomfort of misalignment but moves through it with intention. The kind that treats culture not as a slogan, but as an operating system that must be upgraded if anything else is going to work.

Transformation is not just a project. It's a negotiation

between past, present, and future. And those negotiations don't happen in code—they happen in conversations, in trust, and in the willingness to bridge realities that were never designed to coexist.

THE MYTH OF ALIGNMENT
When agreement isn't the same as understanding

One of the most dangerous assumptions in any transformation effort is that alignment has been achieved simply because agreement has been expressed. People nod in meetings, approve plans, and use the same vocabulary—agility, customer-centricity, innovation—but beneath the surface, their interpretations diverge wildly. What one team calls "minimum viable product," another hears as "cheap and rushed." What one department sees as "empowerment," another interprets as "lack of structure." The result is a mirage of agreement that quickly dissolves once execution begins.

This is the myth of alignment: the belief that shared words equal shared understanding. In practice, alignment is rarely achieved through consensus alone. It requires a far deeper process—one that confronts assumptions, uncovers unspoken fears, and reconciles conflicting definitions of success. And when that process is skipped, the transformation begins on a shaky foundation.

The illusion of alignment often starts with language. Organizations fall in love with certain terms—agile, transformation, innovation—without doing the work of defining them together. The same word becomes a proxy for different meanings depending on who's using it. Leadership may say they want "agile delivery," imagining faster results and fewer escalations. The tech team hears "autonomy and continuous learning." The finance team hears "budget unpredictability." Everyone uses the same word, but they're living in different stories.

This problem is compounded by the structure of most large organizations. Teams are siloed, goals are optimized locally, and success is measured differently across functions. Without intentional alignment, transformation efforts become a patchwork of competing narratives. A platform team focuses on scalability, while a business unit pushes for speed to market. Compliance demands risk reduction, while product design pushes for experimentation. These priorities are not inherently incompatible—but they require alignment at a deeper level than what's usually achieved in status meetings.

Real alignment isn't about surface agreement—it's about shared interpretation. It's about getting to the point where two people in different departments can answer the same question with the same logic, even if they use different language. That level of coherence takes time. It requires structured conversations, not just presentations. It requires listening to what people mean, not just what they say. And most of all, it requires leaders who are willing to slow down and clarify, even when the pressure to execute is high.

When alignment is weak, execution becomes painful. Priorities shift without warning. Dependencies are misunderstood. One team accelerates while another holds back, and friction emerges not because anyone failed, but because no one ever had the same picture of what success looked like. This is when morale drops and trust erodes. People start to disengage, frustrated by what feels like incompetence but is often just misalignment left unaddressed.

Alignment is not a one-time task. It must be maintained, re-clarified, and reinforced as the transformation evolves. New stakeholders join, market conditions shift, strategies pivot. The story must be told again and again, with consistency and with nuance. This storytelling isn't a side activity—it is the work. Because the coherence of a transformation effort lives in the shared story people are moving toward.

I've seen organizations that move slowly but transform successfully, and others that move fast and collapse under misalignment. The difference was never about the quality of the technology or the brilliance of the strategy. It was always about how well people understood each other, how openly they could question assumptions, and how committed they were to staying in sync—not just at kickoff, but every step of the way.

The myth of alignment is seductive because it saves time—at first. But in the long run, skipping this foundational work is one of the costliest mistakes a transformation leader can make. Real alignment is messy. It involves conflict, negotiation, and redefinition. But it's also what makes everything else possible. Without it, transformation becomes a hollow exercise in delivery. With it, it becomes a shared journey—one where people aren't just executing, but moving forward together with purpose and clarity.

SILOS AS SURVIVAL STRATEGIES
Why fragmentation is logical—even when it's harmful

In most organizations, silos are viewed as obstacles to overcome—signs of inefficiency, resistance, or outdated thinking. They're described as barriers to collaboration, innovation, and speed. Transformation initiatives often begin with a mandate to "break down silos," as if they were unnatural flaws in an otherwise healthy system. But this framing misses something important. Silos are not accidental. They are survival strategies—emergent responses to how organizations reward behavior, manage risk, and maintain stability.

To understand why silos persist, we have to stop seeing them as dysfunction and start seeing them as adaptations. People create boundaries because boundaries protect them. Silos offer clarity of role, ownership of resources, control over information. In a complex environment, these things become safety nets. They make the world smaller, more navigable. They allow teams to move at their own pace, define their own success, and shield themselves from the chaos outside.

The problem is not that silos exist. The problem is that they rarely align with how value is actually delivered. Most customer experiences, products, or services require coordination across multiple functions—design, development, legal, operations, compliance, marketing, and more. But when each of these groups operates in its own isolated rhythm, guided by its own metrics and assumptions, the result is fragmentation. Handovers are slow, context is lost, and accountability becomes blurred. Everyone is doing their job, but the outcome doesn't work.

Transformation efforts often stumble here. They

assume that if you change the tools or implement new processes, the silos will naturally dissolve. But silos don't live in tools. They live in relationships, incentives, and unspoken rules. If marketing gets rewarded for brand consistency while product gets rewarded for experimentation, they will pull in opposite directions—no matter how many shared dashboards they have.

This fragmentation becomes most visible when something goes wrong. A delay, a failed release, a compliance issue. Suddenly the silence between silos becomes finger-pointing. Each team explains why it wasn't their fault, how they followed procedure, and why someone else should have flagged the risk. This isn't a moral failure—it's the result of a system that rewards internal optimization over shared responsibility.

To shift this dynamic, leaders must address not just the structure of the organization, but the logic beneath it. What behaviors are we rewarding? What assumptions are baked into our workflows? What risks are teams shielding themselves from, and how can we create new patterns of safety?

Cross-functional collaboration cannot be mandated—it must be made worthwhile. That means creating shared goals that genuinely require cooperation. It means designing processes where success depends on contribution, not isolation. It means telling stories where the hero is not the individual performer, but the integrated team. And it means removing the friction that makes collaboration feel risky or inefficient.

Sometimes this requires changes in tooling, but more often it requires changes in culture. Are people praised for helping other teams succeed? Are timelines realistic enough to allow for genuine coordination? Do leaders model cross-functional alignment, or do they retreat to their own domains when pressure rises?

There's also a personal dimension. In siloed environments, identity is often tied to expertise within a specific function. When transformation begins to blur those lines, people may feel threatened. A developer may resist involving design earlier because it challenges their sense of autonomy. A business analyst may bristle at agile ceremonies that flatten hierarchy. These responses are not resistance to change per se—they are defenses of identity, relevance, and control.

True transformation involves creating new forms of identity that transcend silos. It involves helping people see themselves not just as members of a department, but as contributors to a shared outcome. This doesn't happen through reorganizations alone. It happens through experience—through projects where collaboration pays off, where boundaries blur productively, and where the system begins to feel safer than the silo.

If we want to address silos, we have to stop fighting them directly and start understanding what keeps them alive. Only then can we create the conditions where integration feels less risky than isolation—and where people stop defending their corner and start building together.

LEGACY ISN'T JUST CODE
Why old systems persist and how they shape behavior

When people talk about legacy in the context of transformation, they usually mean systems—aging platforms, outdated databases, brittle infrastructure. But legacy is much more than just code. It's embedded in processes, habits, assumptions, and structures. It lives in how meetings are run, how decisions are made, how success is measured. Legacy is the invisible architecture of the organization—the patterns that persist long after their original purpose has faded.

And the most challenging part? Much of this legacy still works. Or at least, it still produces familiar results. That's why it's so hard to dismantle. Legacy isn't usually broken—it's just misaligned with the future. It's optimized for stability in a world that now demands adaptability. It's efficient in silos, when collaboration is now essential. It assumes control is gained through hierarchy, when today control is earned through trust and clarity.

This is why transformation often feels like swimming against the current. You're not just building something new—you're challenging what has long been considered "how things are done here." And that doesn't just involve systems migration or new tooling. It requires cultural unlearning. And unlearning is harder than learning. It forces people to confront the fact that the methods that once made them successful might no longer be relevant—or worse, might now be the problem.

In this way, legacy becomes a source of identity. People have built their careers within these systems. They've mastered them, navigated them, learned how to get things done through informal workarounds and institutional memory. Asking them to abandon those systems is not just a technical ask—it's a personal one. It implies that the expertise they've spent years cultivating may no longer be valuable. And even if they don't express it, this implication can trigger resistance, doubt, and quiet disengagement.

That's why leading through legacy requires more than technical plans—it requires empathy. You have to understand what people are holding onto and why. You have to recognize that what looks inefficient from the outside may have once been the most elegant solution available. That what seems slow or outdated may, in fact, be a defense against risk, ambiguity, or failure. You're not just updating infrastructure—you're asking people to trust that the new system won't betray them the way the last one sometimes did.

Transformation leaders often make the mistake of treating legacy systems as enemies to be destroyed. But that approach usually backfires. Systems don't respond to hostility—they respond to purpose. If you want people to let go of the old, you have to show them that the new isn't just different, but better. Not better in abstract terms, but better for them—for their work, their users, their ability to contribute meaningfully.

This means involving people early, listening carefully, and designing transitions that honor what came before. It means being clear about what's changing, what's not, and why. And it means resisting the urge to insult the past. Because when people feel that their legacy is being erased rather than evolved, they don't lean into the future—they dig in.

There's also a practical side. Legacy systems often contain dependencies and nuances that no one remembers until they fail. These systems are fragile, but they are also deeply interwoven into business processes. Removing them is not just a technical task—it's an organizational one. It requires mapping, testing, contingency planning, and above all, patience.

So if you're leading transformation and frustrated that things aren't moving faster, ask yourself: what legacy are we really up against? Not just in our systems, but in our thinking, our processes, our expectations?

Legacy isn't just a technical challenge. It's a psychological, political, and emotional one. And until we learn to see it that way, we'll keep underestimating its power—and missing the opportunity to guide people through it with clarity and care. Because transformation doesn't happen when we tear everything down. It happens when we build something so compelling, so useful, and so respectful of where we've been, that people choose to step into what's next.

LEADING THROUGH CULTURAL FRICTION
How to stay effective when nothing feels aligned

Cultural friction is not a sign that something is going wrong in a transformation process—it's a sign that something is finally being revealed. When long-standing assumptions are questioned, when systems are disrupted, and when new ways of working are introduced, friction is inevitable. It's uncomfortable, messy, and often misread as failure. But the leaders who make it through are not those who eliminate friction, but those who learn to work within it.

This is perhaps one of the least taught skills in organizational leadership: how to stay effective when nothing feels aligned. How to move forward when everyone seems to be operating from different maps. How to maintain momentum when your strategy makes sense in theory but is constantly colliding with the way people think, behave, and decide in practice. These moments can feel disorienting. But they are also where leadership becomes real.

Leading through cultural friction begins with awareness. You need to be able to see what's happening underneath the surface. That a stakeholder's reluctance might be fear of losing control. That a team's pushback might be a signal that they haven't been heard. That delays are not always technical—they're often emotional. Cultural patterns are hard to measure, but they are always present. And when you learn to sense them, you begin to understand the real work of transformation: not just building systems, but shifting beliefs.

You can't force this shift. You can't engineer cultural change with a roadmap. What you can do is create the conditions where change becomes possible. This means clarity—about what matters, about what's negotiable and what's not. It means consistency—in how you show up, how you listen, how you communicate. And it means containment—not in the sense of suppression, but in the sense of holding space. Cultural friction produces energy. Your job is to hold that energy, guide it, and use it to fuel forward movement.

There's a kind of leadership that thrives in these conditions. It doesn't rely on positional authority. It doesn't expect perfect alignment. It doesn't chase approval or immediate consensus. Instead, it builds credibility through presence, resilience, and thoughtful action. It learns how to operate in the tension between competing truths. Between what's ideal and what's possible. Between the system as it is and the system as it could be.

When nothing feels aligned, it's tempting to retreat. To simplify the message. To go back to your own silo. To wait for others to come around. But that's precisely when your presence matters most. Cultural transformation is not a sprint. It's a long, uncertain walk in the dark where your ability to model the future—to embody the values and behaviors you want others to adopt—becomes your most powerful tool.

Sometimes this means staying in conversations that are uncomfortable. Sometimes it means being the translator between worlds—between tech and business, legacy and innovation, control and experimentation. Sometimes it means giving people space to catch up, or pulling them gently into the discomfort of change. There is no single playbook. But what remains consistent is your stance— your ability to lead with clarity, integrity, and care even when the environment around you is fragmented.

The leaders who succeed in cultural transformation are not those who push the hardest or shout the loudest. They are the ones who persist. Who stay close to the work, close to the people, and close to the truth. They understand that transformation is not just a shift in tools or structure—it's a shift in collective meaning. And that meaning doesn't change overnight. It evolves, one conversation, one decision, one act of leadership at a time.

So if you find yourself in a space where nothing feels aligned, take a breath. You're not failing. You're in the work. And the work is hard. But it's also necessary. Because alignment doesn't come from removing friction. It comes from moving through it—together, intentionally, and with just enough courage to keep going.

Speed vs. Alignment

HOW URGENCY DESTROYS CLARITY–AND HOW TO
FIX IT

THE ADDICTION TO URGENCY
Why going fast can slow everything down

Modern organizations are addicted to speed. "We need to move faster" has become the default diagnosis for nearly every problem, from sluggish decision-making to delayed product launches. Velocity is not just a goal—it's a culture, a mindset, almost a moral imperative. And yet, many of the transformation efforts I've witnessed that failed or stalled did so not because they moved too slowly, but because they moved too fast.

Speed feels good. It signals decisiveness, ambition, competitiveness. It creates a sense of momentum and confidence. When leadership insists on fast timelines and aggressive milestones, it gives the impression that things are under control. But beneath the surface, the pressure to move quickly often sacrifices the very things that make transformation successful: alignment, clarity, quality, and trust.

What begins as a drive for momentum can quickly

become chaos in disguise. Teams sprint without direction, delivering outputs with little understanding of their purpose. Critical conversations are skipped in favor of progress reports. Decision-making becomes reactive. People become more concerned with appearing fast than being effective. Metrics are gamed. Tensions rise. And soon, speed becomes a mask for disconnection.

There's also a psychological trap in urgency. It creates the illusion of importance. When everything is urgent, everything feels essential. But in reality, urgency is often a substitute for priority. Teams are overwhelmed not because they have too much to do, but because no one has taken the time to define what truly matters. When timelines are arbitrary, when goals are vague, when deliverables are pushed without context, speed creates confusion, not clarity.

This urgency addiction is often reinforced from the top. Leaders feel pressure to show results—especially in trans-formation programs where budgets are high and expecta-tions are higher. So they compress timelines, demand quick wins, and celebrate activity over insight. They ask for roadmaps before discovery is complete. They push for delivery without alignment. And then they're surprised when the results don't match the ambition.

It's important to say: speed itself isn't the problem. The problem is *unfocused* speed—movement without meaning. True velocity comes from coherence, from aligned teams working toward a clear goal with the autonomy to make decisions. In that environment, teams can move fast *and* well. But getting there requires slowing down—at least at the start.

One of the most valuable skills in transformation is knowing when to pause. When to ask the hard questions. When to make space for alignment. When to clarify before you build. This kind of discipline often feels countercultural in fast-moving organizations. It can look like indecision or hesitation. But in truth, it's the foundation of sustainable speed. Because when teams are clear on what matters, they don't need to waste time negotiating priorities or cleaning up avoidable mistakes. They just move.

There's also a human cost to urgency that is rarely acknowledged. People burn out, not because they're unwilling to work hard, but because they're forced to work fast without context or agency. The pressure to deliver quickly without understanding the "why" creates disengagement. It turns talented people into frustrated executors. And over time, it erodes the trust and creativity that transformation desperately needs.

To shift out of the urgency trap, leaders must redefine what speed means. It's not about checking boxes. It's not about being the first to market at any cost. It's about reducing waste—not just in process, but in decision-making, alignment, and communication. It's about accelerating the *right* things, and letting go of the need to rush the rest.

Transformation isn't a race—it's a recalibration. It asks us to move at the pace of understanding, not pressure. To lead with intention, not haste. And to remember that real progress is not measured by how fast we move, but by how clearly we know where we're going.

FALSE STARTS AND FORCED MARCHES
How rushing alignment leads to wasted motion

One of the most common failure patterns in digital transformation is the false start. It looks like momentum—teams are assembled, timelines are set, slides are presented, and delivery begins. But beneath the surface, the foundations are shaky. Alignment hasn't truly been reached. Critical questions remain unanswered. The "why" of the work is unclear or contested. Still, the machine moves forward, propelled by urgency, political pressure, or sheer inertia. It looks like action, but it's really motion without traction.

These false starts are not harmless. They consume attention, burn budget, and drain credibility. Worse, they create cynicism. Teams begin to believe that change is performative. That strategy shifts are temporary. That today's urgent project will be tomorrow's forgotten experiment. Every new initiative feels like a rebranding of the last one, with new language but the same lack of clarity. And when that pattern repeats, people stop investing themselves. They deliver what's asked, but nothing more. The spark is gone.

This is what happens when alignment is rushed. It's not that people resist alignment—they simply aren't given the space or time to reach it. Decisions are made in narrow rooms. Goals are defined without input. Cross-functional conversations are compressed or skipped. Assumptions are baked into plans without being tested. There's no time to check for shared understanding, so the illusion of consensus is treated as fact.

What follows is often a forced march. Teams are asked to deliver at speed under constraints they didn't help define. Conflicts emerge not because people are uncooperative, but because their perspectives were never integrated.

Dependencies are revealed too late. Priorities shift midstream. Feedback loops are weak or non-existent. Yet the project continues, pushed forward by momentum rather than clarity. Everyone is busy, but no one is confident.

The irony is that these failures are often predictable. The warning signs are there from the beginning: ambiguous scope, too many "TBDs," misaligned stakeholders, a lack of real sponsorship. But in the rush to start, these signs are ignored or minimized. Optimism replaces inquiry. Delivery begins before readiness is confirmed. And by the time the cracks appear, the cost of slowing down feels even higher—so the project pushes on, increasingly brittle and fragile.

The cost of false starts is not just financial. It's cultural. It reinforces the idea that strategy is disconnected from execution. That plans are made elsewhere, by others. That feedback is a formality, not a loop. These are not just project risks—they're cultural infections. And once embedded, they make every future transformation harder to trust, harder to fund, and harder to lead.

Avoiding false starts means resisting the pressure to begin before you're ready. It means treating alignment not as a box to check, but as a condition to satisfy. It means asking the uncomfortable questions early—What problem are we solving? Who owns the outcome? What does success really look like? Where are the tensions, the blind spots, the unresolved assumptions? These questions don't delay the work—they *are* the work.

It also means slowing down to speed up. Taking the time to map stakeholders, clarify intent, and build a shared narrative pays off later in speed, trust, and reduced rework. Teams that align early are more autonomous. They don't need to escalate decisions or constantly renegotiate scope.

They can adapt in real time because they're anchored in shared understanding.

Leadership plays a crucial role here. Leaders must create the permission to pause. To question. To surface disagreement before it becomes conflict. They must reward clarity over urgency and model the discipline of alignment, even when it feels slow. Because when leaders prioritize alignment, they make it safe for others to do the same.

False starts don't happen because people don't care. They happen because systems reward motion over meaning. If we want real change, we need to flip that equation. Start not with speed, but with understanding. Not with plans, but with purpose. That's how you avoid marching fast in the wrong direction—and start moving with intention toward something that matters.

SPEED WITHOUT STRATEGY
Why movement doesn't equal momentum

There's a kind of electricity that runs through organizations when a big initiative is launched. Calendars fill up, plans are drafted, messages go out. Everyone feels the urgency—something is moving, finally. There's talk of "quick wins," "lean execution," and "hitting the ground running." Leaders push for results. Teams scramble to deliver. And at first, this burst of activity feels like progress.

But not all movement is forward. Sometimes, speed masks the absence of strategy.

When urgency takes over, clarity often disappears. Instead of asking the right questions, teams default to action. Instead of aligning on purpose, they align on deadlines. The focus shifts from *why* we're doing something to *how fast* we can get it out the door. Strategy becomes a background hum, barely audible under the roar of deliverables.

It doesn't happen because people are careless. It happens because modern work teaches us to associate momentum with value. Shipping something, anything, feels better than pausing to reflect. Stopping, even briefly, can seem like weakness—or worse, irrelevance. So teams move. They build. They iterate. But often, they do it without a shared understanding of the goal.

And when that shared understanding is missing, the cost is rarely immediate. In the short term, things look productive. Dashboards light up. Timelines stay intact. But over time, misalignment starts to show. The product doesn't quite solve the problem it was meant to address. The new process creates confusion instead of clarity. The "transformation" feels disconnected from day-to-day work.

You can see it in the small things. A team completes a

major delivery but can't articulate how it ties back to the strategy. Stakeholders nod in meetings but walk away with different interpretations. Roadmaps shift not because of insight, but because someone senior changed their mind. The organization keeps moving, but the direction is fuzzy. And eventually, that fuzziness turns into friction.

Friction, in this context, doesn't always show up as conflict. More often, it shows up as fatigue. People feel like they're running hard but not getting anywhere. Morale dips. Creativity flattens. Teams stop questioning the value of their work and start focusing on surviving the next sprint, the next deadline, the next review. The initial energy that came with the push for speed is replaced by quiet cynicism.

The most ironic part is that true speed—the kind that delivers real value—is almost impossible without strategy. When teams are clear on what they're trying to achieve and why it matters, they make better decisions faster. They need fewer meetings. They argue less about priorities. They spend less time fixing work that was misdirected. In other words, alignment is a multiplier. Without it, speed turns chaotic. With it, momentum becomes sustainable.

Yet, in many organizations, strategy is treated as a luxury—something reserved for offsites, slide decks, or yearly planning sessions. It's rarely woven into the rhythm of execution. As a result, teams are left to interpret it on their own, often without context or clarity. Some guess. Some improvise. Some just stop asking.

Reversing this pattern doesn't require slowing everything down. It requires creating intentional pauses. Moments to realign. Space to ask uncomfortable questions before the next big push. It means treating strategy not as a static document, but as a living conversation—one that teams revisit and reshape as they learn. It means equipping people with not just roadmaps, but with the context to make tradeoffs that matter.

The best teams don't reject speed. They redefine it. They understand that going fast in the wrong direction is just wasted energy. They know that clarity is not a blocker, but a catalyst. And they fight for it—not by resisting urgency, but by anchoring it in something deeper.

In these teams, speed doesn't mean hustle without thought. It means confidence without chaos. It means fewer detours. Fewer "redo" moments. Fewer meetings to align after the damage is done. Because alignment isn't a tax—it's an investment in going faster *and* smarter.

Real transformation doesn't come from chasing velocity. It comes from creating velocity that's grounded in purpose. Without that, even the most disciplined execution ends up as noise.

ALIGNMENT IS A FORCE MULTIPLIER
How shared understanding creates real velocity

Alignment isn't just a soft skill or a leadership buzzword—it's the most underestimated accelerant in any transformation. When people are truly aligned, decisions happen faster. Workflows become smoother. Meetings shrink. Teams take initiative because they don't have to wait for instructions or second-guess intentions. The time normally spent clarifying, escalating, or redoing is reclaimed for actual progress. In this way, alignment is not the opposite of speed—it is what enables it.

Yet in most organizations, alignment is treated as a luxury. Something we hope for, but don't make time for. When deadlines loom, when pressure mounts, the instinct is to cut corners, to push forward and "figure it out later." But later rarely arrives. Misalignment, once embedded, spreads like a quiet virus. It shows up in the way teams interpret goals differently. In how priorities are debated rather than executed. In the way momentum slows to a crawl, even as everyone appears busy.

The reason alignment works as a force multiplier is simple: it reduces friction. When everyone shares a clear understanding of what matters, ambiguity dissolves. People make better micro-decisions, which means fewer macro-corrections. They coordinate more intuitively, because they're anchored in a common purpose. They speak the same strategic language, which reduces misunderstandings and rework. Trust increases, because intentions are clearer and less contested. And with trust comes the ability to move faster, with less oversight and fewer defensive behaviors.

Alignment also reduces emotional drag. When people know what they're working toward—and why—they worry less. They don't have to navigate the fog of organizational politics or decode vague priorities. They don't have to protect themselves from being blamed for guessing wrong. This cognitive and emotional clarity translates into energy, engagement, and flow. The team becomes more than the sum of its parts.

But alignment is not something you achieve once and then move on. It's a living state. It must be nurtured, recalibrated, and protected. As transformation unfolds, the landscape changes. Priorities shift, new actors emerge, constraints evolve. What was once clear becomes contested. That's why alignment must be designed into the rhythm of the work. It must be revisited, not just in retrospectives or quarterly reviews, but in the day-to-day mechanics of leadership.

Leaders who treat alignment as a continual responsibility, rather than a one-time event, build systems that are faster by design. They ask clarifying questions early. They listen for divergence before it becomes conflict. They invest in shared language and common reference points. And they make alignment visible—so that when it begins to fray, it can be addressed quickly rather than discovered too late.

This doesn't mean constant consensus. In fact, alignment is often built through disagreement—through surfacing different perspectives and working through them until a stronger shared direction emerges. It's not about pleasing everyone or reaching uniformity. It's about coherence. About ensuring that, even if people don't fully agree, they understand the path and are willing to move forward on it together.

One of the clearest signs of alignment is speed with confidence. When teams don't just act quickly, but know why they're acting—and feel supported in that action.

When decisions can be made without escalating because the principles are understood. When risks are flagged early, because there's enough clarity and trust to raise concerns without fear.

This kind of velocity can't be manufactured through pressure. It can't be faked with dashboards or forced through deadlines. It has to be built. Through dialogue. Through clarity. Through leadership that values direction as much as motion.

If you want speed, don't start by pushing harder. Start by aligning better. The real accelerators in transformation aren't more tools or more processes—they're people who know where they're going, why it matters, and how to get there together. That's alignment. And that's how speed becomes not just faster, but smarter.

CHOOSING CLARITY OVER SPEED
How intentional pause leads to meaningful progress

In moments of pressure, leaders often face a choice: do we keep pushing forward in the name of speed, or do we pause to clarify before continuing? The instinct, especially in environments driven by urgency and visibility, is to push. Stopping feels risky. It looks like delay. It can be hard to justify. But some of the most effective and impactful transformation work I've seen came not from acceleration, but from a well-timed pause. A moment where someone chose clarity over speed—and changed the trajectory of the entire effort as a result.

Clarity doesn't mean overthinking. It doesn't mean paralysis. It means being willing to ask the hard questions before the system is too far in motion to change direction. What are we really trying to achieve? Who owns this decision? What assumptions are we making that haven't been tested? What impact are we hoping to create, and how will we know if we're getting closer?

These questions often surface discomfort. They slow things down. They force people to confront ambiguity and admit what they don't yet know. But this discomfort is productive. It reveals gaps before they become failures. It surfaces disagreements while they can still be resolved constructively. It gives people the language and confidence they need to act with intention, not just urgency.

In many cases, the cost of this pause is tiny compared to the cost of moving fast in the wrong direction. A week of clarification can prevent six months of rework. One honest conversation can dissolve months of passive conflict. One shared document, thoughtfully written and discussed, can align teams that would otherwise drift apart under pressure. Yet despite this, pausing still feels counter-cultural in many organizations—almost like an act of defiance.

That's why choosing clarity requires courage. It means challenging the belief that more activity equals more value. It means being the person who says, "We're not ready yet," not because of fear, but because of responsibility. It means taking the long view, even when the short-term demands feel louder.

Clarity is not about being slow. It's about making sure that speed, when it comes, is real. That teams are not just busy, but effective. That what's being delivered is meaningful, not just measurable. And that the energy being spent is actually moving the organization closer to its goals, not just deeper into its backlog.

It also creates emotional safety. When people are clear on direction, on purpose, on priorities, they're less anxious. They don't waste energy second-guessing or covering themselves. They collaborate more easily, because they're not trying to protect themselves from ambiguity. And they're more willing to raise concerns early, because they trust that the team is listening. In this way, clarity becomes not just a strategic asset, but a cultural one.

As a leader, your ability to create clarity sets the tone for everything else. It shapes how people interpret change, how they respond to uncertainty, and how they treat each other under pressure. And the best leaders I've worked with are not the ones who always have the answers. They're the ones who know how to create the space for better questions.

So before you rush into your next transformation sprint, ask yourself: what's missing? What doesn't feel aligned? What conversations haven't happened yet? And most importantly: are we moving because we're ready, or because we're afraid to slow down?

Choosing clarity over speed doesn't mean you'll never go fast. It means that when you do, it will matter. Because your speed will be anchored in shared understanding, thoughtful intent, and a strategy that your entire team believes in—not just follows.

Transformation isn't a race. It's a shared journey through complexity. And sometimes, the most powerful move you can make is not forward—but deeper. Into purpose, into context, into clarity. That's how progress becomes real. That's how momentum becomes sustainable. And that's how leadership becomes meaningful.

PART II
Building the Foundation for Change

TOOLS, MINDSETS, AND CONVERSATIONS THAT MAKE CHANGE POSSIBLE

If the previous part was about confronting the hidden forces that sabotage transformation, Part II is about creating the conditions that make it work. This is where we shift from awareness to action—from diagnosing the dysfunction to building the foundation for meaningful, lasting change.

And make no mistake: foundations matter.

In the rush to deliver, many organizations skip this phase. They jump straight into delivery mode, launching sprints, purchasing new tools, rebranding initiatives as "digital," and expecting things to improve. But if the underlying conditions aren't there—if the culture, the incentives, the mindsets, and the relationships aren't aligned—then no tool, no framework, no executive push will be enough. The work will look good on the surface but remain fragile underneath. And in time, the cracks will show.

This part of the book is about doing the slower, deeper

work. It's about establishing the elements that allow teams to operate with clarity and resilience in the face of constant change. Not process for the sake of process—but thoughtful scaffolding that supports autonomy. Not communication theatre—but real dialogue that builds trust and unlocks insight. Not generic leadership advice—but grounded practices that work for those who are leading from the middle.

We begin with the role of those leaders. Not executives. Not consultants. But the people in the middle of the system—the product owners, project leads, delivery managers, and change agents who are asked to influence without authority, drive progress across silos, and keep things moving while everything around them shifts. These are the people transformation depends on. And too often, they're overlooked, under-supported, and left to figure things out alone.

From there, we examine a critical shift in thinking: from output to outcome. The difference may sound subtle, but it changes everything. When we define success by what we produce instead of the impact we create, we end up chasing activity instead of value. Shifting to an outcome mindset means asking harder questions, involving the right people earlier, and being willing to change course when new information emerges. It also means letting go of false precision and embracing continuous learning.

The third chapter in this part explores what it means to design for humans—not personas, not workflows, but real people navigating real complexity. Too often, transformation is built around abstract models. But abstraction creates distance, and distance creates failure. When we learn to design with empathy, to think in systems, and to remove friction instead of adding layers of control, we begin to create experiences that actually work.

Taken together, these three chapters offer a blueprint—not a formula—for building change-ready environments. They won't give you a perfect process. But they will help you ask better questions, design better conversations, and lead more intentionally.

The foundation of transformation is not digital. It's relational. It's built in trust, in clarity, in shared under-standing. These aren't nice-to-haves. They're the infrastructure of progress. Without them, change becomes a slogan. With them, it becomes a capability.

If you've ever felt stuck between strategy and delivery, if you've ever tried to lead without authority, if you've ever felt the friction between ambition and reality—this part is for you.

Leading from the Middle

POWER, INFLUENCE, AND DECISION-MAKING
WITHOUT AUTHORITY

THE INVISIBLE POSITION
What it really means to lead without being in charge

There's a particular type of leadership that doesn't come with a title, a corner office, or a mandate. It lives in the middle of the organization—between teams, between domains, between agendas. It's the kind of leadership exercised by people who are responsible for outcomes but don't have the formal authority to make all the decisions. Product owners, project leads, delivery managers, team facilitators—these are the roles that keep transformation alive. Not by commanding, but by connecting.

Leading from the middle is rarely glamorous. It means being the translator between vision and execution. It means holding the space when strategy is unclear. It means listening more than speaking, influencing more than dictating, and navigating power dynamics that are often unspoken. And yet, it's in these middle spaces that real change is shaped—not by decree, but through dialogue, alignment, and persistence.

What makes this kind of leadership so challenging is also what makes it so valuable. The middle is messy. You're close enough to the work to see what's broken, but not always close enough to fix it yourself. You're expected to align teams, but those teams don't report to you. You're asked to deliver outcomes, but the goals shift mid-project. You're caught between the needs of the people doing the work and the expectations of the people funding it.

And still, the work gets done—because someone in the middle keeps it moving.

But let's be honest: it's exhausting. It's a role that comes with enormous emotional labor. You have to absorb frustration, manage uncertainty, and maintain momentum in systems that weren't designed to be fast or flexible. You don't get the credit when things go well, and you often carry the blame when they don't. And yet, organizations depend on you. Not just to deliver, but to sense, interpret, and bridge the gaps that others don't even see.

The power of the middle lies in its perspective. You see across silos. You notice patterns that others miss. You understand both the strategic and the operational, because you live at the intersection of the two. That perspective is incredibly valuable—but only if it's activated. Too often, people in the middle underestimate their influence. They wait for permission. They assume someone else will make the call. They silence their insight in the name of "staying in their lane."

But in complex systems, waiting for clarity is a luxury. Leadership from the middle means stepping into the ambiguity and choosing to act—not recklessly, but intentionally. It means influencing without authority by building trust, framing problems clearly, and creating momentum that others can align to. It means asking better questions, modeling better behavior, and becoming the connective tissue that helps the system evolve.

You don't need a title to lead. What you need is presence, clarity, and a deep understanding of how decisions actually get made—not just on paper, but in the hallways, the Slack threads, the side conversations. Power in organizations is rarely linear. It moves through relationships, stories, and timing. When you learn how to read that power, and how to navigate it with integrity, you become not just a contributor—but a catalyst.

This chapter is about reclaiming the agency that so many people in the middle give away. It's about understanding the unique leverage you have—not because of where you sit in the hierarchy, but because of what you see and how you show up. It's about shifting from "I don't have the authority" to "I have access, insight, and influence —and I intend to use them."

Because in today's organizations, the people who lead transformation are not always the ones with the most power. They're the ones who know how to use the power they have—quietly, wisely, and persistently. That's leadership from the middle. And it's more necessary than ever.

INFLUENCE WITHOUT PERMISSION
How trust, framing, and consistency build informal power

If you're leading from the middle, chances are no one gave you a formal green light to shape the direction of change. You weren't handed a mandate or a team of direct reports. Instead, you were likely handed ambiguity, a pile of dependencies, and an implicit expectation to "make things happen." In that context, authority is scarce—but influence is everything. And influence doesn't require permission. It requires presence, intention, and trust.

Influence without authority often begins with trust, but trust isn't built through generic positivity or empty promises. It's built through reliability. When you consistently show up prepared, ask thoughtful questions, listen actively, and follow through on what you say, people start to rely on you. Over time, that reliability turns into credibility—and credibility becomes a form of power. Not because you can compel action, but because people want to work with you. They believe you add clarity, reduce friction, and move things forward.

That's the foundation. But to scale that influence, you need more than just reliability—you need framing. In the chaos of transformation, people crave orientation. They want to understand why things are happening, how decisions are being made, and what they're supposed to care about. Most environments don't provide this clarity. That's where you come in. If you can articulate the landscape—make sense of competing priorities, name tensions that others avoid, and connect the dots between strategy and execution—you quickly become someone others look to for guidance.

Framing is not about being the smartest person in the

room. It's about noticing what's missing and supplying it. Sometimes that's context. Sometimes it's language. Sometimes it's just the courage to name the thing that no one wants to say. When you do this consistently, you begin to shape the narrative—and narratives are how organizations make decisions. This is influence at its most subtle, and its most powerful.

Consistency is the third pillar. Influence fades without it. If people have to guess which version of you they're getting in every meeting, they won't trust you. If your standards shift depending on the audience, your credibility weakens. But when you show up with the same clarity, tone, and integrity—regardless of pressure—you create a gravitational pull. People lean in. They know what to expect. And they start to align with you, even if you don't have formal authority.

One of the traps in leading without authority is the temptation to over-rely on charm, persuasion, or consensus. But influence isn't about being liked—it's about being useful. You earn influence by reducing uncertainty, enabling progress, and helping others succeed. Sometimes that means disagreeing. Sometimes it means holding the line. Influence without a point of view is just noise. Influence with clarity is leadership.

You also have to be strategic about where you invest it. Not every battle is worth fighting. Not every disagreement needs resolution. When you lead from the middle, your energy is limited—and your credibility is tied to how you use it. Choose moments that matter. Speak up when the cost of silence is high. Push when the system needs a nudge, and pause when it needs space. The timing of your influence is often more important than the content.

Finally, remember that influence compounds. Every interaction is a deposit in the trust bank. Every decision framed well, every hard truth spoken calmly, every messy moment handled with grace—it all adds up. You may not feel powerful in the moment, but others are noticing. Your ability to lead will not come from a promotion or a reorg. It will come from a quiet accumulation of trust, clarity, and action.

So if you're waiting for permission to lead—stop. You already have more influence than you think. And if you start using it with intention, you'll find that even in the most complex systems, change begins to move—not because someone told it to, but because you showed what was possible.

REFRAMING DECISION-MAKING
Moving from gatekeeping to guidance

One of the most frustrating experiences for anyone leading from the middle is watching decisions get stuck. Meetings end without clarity, dependencies pile up, and the same discussions repeat with different people and no forward motion. It's not that no one cares—it's that decision-making in most organizations is designed around authority, not flow. And when authority is unclear or distributed, the system seizes up.

If you don't hold formal power, you can't force decisions. But you can reshape how decisions are approached —and that, in itself, is a kind of leadership. Instead of trying to control decisions, you become the person who clarifies them. You reframe the process from one of gatekeeping—who gets to say yes—to one of guidance—what would make this a clear yes for the right people.

This shift begins with how decisions are framed. Most decisions are presented too early or too vaguely. Stakeholders are brought in without enough context or too much ambiguity. When people feel rushed or confused, they default to delay. The decision is postponed "until we know more," or "until X signs off," and another week slips by.

You can prevent this by anticipating what good decision-making looks like. What information is missing? What trade-offs are on the table? Who will be affected? What are the criteria for success? When you do this thinking upfront, and bring clarity instead of just requests, you make it easier for decision-makers to act.

This doesn't mean doing the work for them—it means lowering the cognitive load. Leaders are often overwhelmed, context-switching, and managing multiple pressures. When you become the person who simplifies the decision, instead of just escalating it, you become a trusted partner rather than another point of noise.

You also shift the conversation from "Who has the power to decide?" to "What conditions make this decision easier?" That's a very different conversation. One is about authority; the other is about clarity. One puts people on the defensive; the other invites collaboration. When you create that shift, you unlock movement. The system doesn't need a hero. It needs a facilitator of flow.

Another aspect of reframing decision-making is expanding the definition of influence. Decisions in organizations are rarely made in a single moment. They are shaped in side conversations, through informal coalitions, and via the quiet politics of timing. When you understand this, you stop waiting for the "official" meeting and start preparing the ground beforehand—listening, seeding ideas, gathering support. You turn decision-making from a single point into a process—and that process becomes your leverage.

It also means accepting that some decisions are slow for a reason. Risk, reputation, compliance, politics—all of these are real. But even within those constraints, you can shift the tone. You can frame the risk in human terms. You can define minimum viable progress. You can offer options instead of ultimatums. You can show what happens if we don't decide—what the cost of inaction really is.

Leading from the middle isn't about pushing people into decisions—they'll resist that. It's about creating an environment where decisions feel safer, clearer, and more inevitable. That takes discipline, empathy, and patience. It means knowing when to nudge, when to hold back, and when to simply make the next move yourself, within the scope you control.

Ultimately, decision-making isn't a bottleneck because people are indecisive. It's a bottleneck because the system doesn't make it easy to be decisive. Your role isn't to fix that system overnight—but to hack it with clarity. To become the person who helps others see the decision more clearly, feel more confident in making it, and understand the impact of delaying it.

When you reframe decision-making this way, you don't just move projects forward. You change the energy of the room. You help people stop waiting for permission and start acting with intent. And that shift—small as it seems— is the difference between stuck and unstuck, between inertia and progress.

DEALING WITH RESISTANCE AND POLITICS
Staying effective without getting cynical

If you're leading from the middle, sooner or later you'll run into resistance—not the loud, obvious kind, but the quiet, structural kind. It's in the passive-aggressive meeting replies, the silent rejections, the priorities that shift without warning. It's in the way some leaders delay without saying no, and others say yes without ever following through. It's in the organizational politics you didn't ask to play, but can't afford to ignore. And if you're not prepared for it, this resistance can wear you down.

Let's be clear: resistance is not failure. It's feedback. And politics are not a distraction—they're the medium through which most influence travels. Leading from the middle means understanding both, navigating both, and doing so without losing your edge or your optimism.

Resistance usually isn't about you. It's about risk. When people push back, stall, or disappear, they're often protecting themselves—sometimes from visible conse- quences, sometimes from emotional discomfort. Your initiative might challenge their priorities, their budget, their domain of control, or simply their sense of safety in a changing system. Understanding this helps you shift from frustration to curiosity. Instead of "Why are they blocking me?" you start asking, "What are they protecting, and how can I speak to that?"

In this way, resistance becomes a signal, not an obsta- cle. It shows you where the system is fragile, where align- ment is missing, where fear lives. And once you understand that, you can adapt—not by backing down, but by engaging more intelligently. You reframe your pitch. You speak their language. You shift from pushing an idea to solving a shared problem. You don't compromise your goals—you recalibrate your approach.

This is where politics come in—not as manipulation, but as awareness. Organizational politics are simply the informal rules by which influence flows. Power isn't always where the org chart says it is. Sometimes it's in legacy relationships, unofficial advisors, or internal reputations that no one talks about but everyone respects. If you ignore these dynamics, you'll waste time speaking to authority without speaking to power.

So you learn. You map the landscape. You listen more than you speak, especially early on. You pay attention to who people defer to, who they mention, who they avoid. You track how decisions actually get made—not how the process is described, but how it unfolds. And then you move within that reality, not in opposition to it.

It's tempting, when faced with enough resistance, to check out emotionally. To become cynical. To retreat into your lane and stop caring about the bigger picture. But cynicism is just burnout with a sharper vocabulary. It makes you feel smarter, but it reduces your impact. Staying effective means staying connected—to purpose, to people, to progress—even when the system is slow to respond.

This doesn't mean being naive. It means being resilient. You pick your battles. You focus on what you can control. You celebrate small wins—not because they're enough, but because they keep you and your team moving. You vent when you need to, but you don't let frustration shape your behavior. You remember that you're playing a long game—and that even small changes in complex systems can have outsized effects over time.

Above all, you resist the temptation to become the system you're trying to change. Just because others operate through avoidance or self-interest doesn't mean you have to. Your clarity, your curiosity, your consistency—these are your tools. They're how you lead through resistance without becoming resistant yourself.

There's no playbook for navigating politics and push-back. But there is a mindset: open, observant, intentional. If you can hold onto that—if you can keep showing up, keep asking better questions, and keep moving with purpose—you'll find that even in the messiest environments, influence grows. And eventually, so does trust. That's what opens doors. That's what creates space. And that's what allows you to lead—not despite resistance, but through it.

CREATING YOUR OWN CENTER OF GRAVITY
Becoming the steady point others can organize around

When you lead from the middle, you're often surrounded by turbulence—shifting priorities, partial information, unclear roles, and mixed signals from leadership. It's easy to become reactive in that environment, constantly adjusting to everyone else's needs, decisions, and emotions. But there's another option, one that changes everything: become the stable point. The reference others start to use when everything else feels uncertain.

This is what it means to create your own center of gravity. It doesn't mean being inflexible. It means being anchored. It means having a clear sense of what matters, what you're building toward, and how you make decisions —so that others begin to orient around your clarity, your calm, and your consistency.

In chaotic systems, people naturally gravitate toward signals of coherence. They want someone who can explain what's happening, not perfectly, but clearly. Someone who remembers the purpose when others forget. Someone who doesn't escalate every issue, but helps resolve them. When you become that person, you don't just gain credibility— you create alignment. Not through authority, but through presence.

This isn't about having all the answers. It's about having a posture. A way of engaging that others trust. You take the time to understand before reacting. You check your assumptions. You explain your thinking. You communicate early and often, even when there's nothing "final" to say. You're not the loudest person in the room, but you're the one people look to when things start to wobble.

Over time, that stability becomes power—not the kind

that comes from hierarchy, but the kind that comes from reputation. People come to you not just for status updates, but for perspective. They ask for your input in high-stakes moments, not because you control the outcome, but because you've shown you can hold complexity without making it heavier.

This kind of influence is slow to build, but incredibly hard to replace. It doesn't require you to control others—it requires you to manage yourself. To be intentional with your attention. To protect your energy. To say no when necessary. To maintain your values even when it would be easier not to. And in doing so, you become the person others count on when the noise is loud and the path isn't clear.

Creating your own center of gravity also means staying connected to purpose. Not just the company's goals, but your own. Why are you here? What does meaningful progress look like for you? What kind of culture are you trying to shape, regardless of whether you have permission to change it? Purpose isn't always handed to you. Sometimes you have to define it yourself, and let that definition guide your behavior.

And here's the paradox: when you act with that kind of internal clarity, your external impact increases. People trust those who know where they stand. They follow those who move with intention. And they align with those who show, through their actions, that leadership doesn't require a title —just courage, consistency, and care.

So when everything around you feels in motion, don't just react. Ground yourself. Name what matters. Lead with clarity. And trust that in doing so, you're not just surviving complexity—you're shaping how others move through it too.

That's what it means to lead from the middle. Not by

waiting to be empowered, but by becoming a source of stability, focus, and momentum. You're not just pat of the system. You're shaping it, one interaction at a time. And over time, that gravity becomes real—something others can feel, follow, and rely on.

From Output to Outcome

REDEFINING SUCCESS IN TRANSFORMATION

THE FALLACY OF DONE
Why shipping doesn't mean succeeding

In most organizations, "done" is a sacred word. It signals progress, completion, certainty. Teams race toward it. Leaders demand it. Reports are filled with it. We shipped the feature. We completed the migration. We hit the milestone. Done means something happened. But in digital transformation, *done* doesn't mean what we think it does. In fact, it can be one of the most misleading signals in the system.

That's because transformation isn't about what gets shipped—it's about what changes. And those are not the same thing.

Shipping a product doesn't guarantee adoption. Completing a project doesn't mean it created value. Finishing a process redesign doesn't ensure that people actually use it, or that it makes their lives better. These are output-based definitions of success. They measure activity, not impact. They tell us that work occurred—not whether it mattered.

The fallacy of done is seductive because it's measurable. You can track outputs. You can report them. You can put them in a slide deck and say, "Look, we're making progress." But progress toward *what?* When we mistake outputs for outcomes, we risk building faster than we can learn. We reward motion, not value. We celebrate completion over consequence.

This is especially true in environments where pressure is high. Leaders want to show momentum. Teams want to protect themselves from scrutiny. So everyone gravitates toward the work that looks good on paper. Roadmaps become delivery schedules, not learning journeys. And before long, transformation is reduced to a checklist—each item marked "done" while the underlying problems remain untouched.

The danger here isn't just wasted effort—it's lost credibility. When outputs don't lead to real change, people start to disengage. Stakeholders become skeptical. End users stop trusting the process. Teams get cynical. And the transformation loses its moral center. It becomes something we perform, not something we pursue.

So what does it mean to move beyond done? It starts with redefining what success looks like. Not as a deliverable, but as a shift. A new behavior. A measurable improvement in how something works. Maybe it's reduced time-to-value for customers. Maybe it's fewer support tickets, more cross-team collaboration, or better decisions made closer to the edge. Whatever it is, it needs to be *felt*—by someone, somewhere, in the real world of work.

This shift requires courage. It's easier to promise features than outcomes. Easier to manage scope than to manage meaning. But if we want transformation to be more than cosmetic, we have to resist the illusion of done. We have to ask harder questions: Who benefits from this? What will be different because of it? How will we know if it worked?

It also requires new rhythms. Feedback cycles. Loops of learning. Mechanisms to test assumptions, gather insight, and adapt in real time. Transformation can't be a one-way street from strategy to execution. It has to be a conversation—between intention and reality, between what we build and how it behaves.

Done is not the enemy. But it's not the destination either. It's a checkpoint. A pause. A moment to ask, *what now?* Did this thing we built help someone do something better? Did it bring us closer to the world we're trying to create? Or did we just move the work forward without moving the system?

These are uncomfortable questions. But they're also the most important ones. Because transformation isn't just about building. It's about becoming. And becoming takes more than getting things done. It takes knowing why they matter. And caring enough to find out.

DEFINING VALUE WITHOUT VANITY
How to measure what matters (and stop pretending otherwise)

In the language of transformation, few words are used more and understood less than *value*. It appears on every roadmap, strategy slide, and OKR document. Deliver value. Maximize value. Prioritize high-value work. But ask a team what *value* actually means in their context—and you'll get either a long pause or a dozen different answers. That ambiguity is not harmless. It's the reason why so many organizations deliver features that don't get used, redesign processes no one adopts, and optimize for metrics that impress on paper but mean little in practice.

To move from output to outcome, we need to stop hiding behind the word *value* and start defining it—specifically, honestly, and contextually.

First, let's acknowledge that most organizations already have value metrics—but many of them are vanity metrics. They look good. They trend upward. They're easy to report. But they don't tell the truth. Page views. Number of meetings held. Tickets closed. Features released. Hours logged. These are proxies, not proof. They describe activity, not improvement.

Vanity metrics aren't inherently bad—they can signal movement. But when they become the definition of success, the system gets distorted. Teams start optimizing for what's measurable instead of what matters. They design for the dashboard, not for the user. And leadership, in turn, begins to believe the story they see in reports—while the real pain points go unaddressed.

Redefining value starts with asking: *valuable to whom?* And for what purpose? A new workflow might reduce steps, but if it increases confusion, is that a win? A faster

73

release cycle might sound good, but if no one adopts the new functionality, what's the gain? A high engagement score might feel like success, but if people are just clicking without acting, what does it mean?

These questions require us to shift from *output-focused metrics* to *impact-focused learning.* Instead of "Did we deliver what we planned?" we ask, "Did anything get better because of it?" And instead of pretending we know what matters upfront, we design mechanisms to find out. We talk to real users. We measure behavior change. We look for friction reduced, time saved, confidence increased. And we make space to be surprised.

This also means involving the right voices. Value is often defined at a distance—from the top of the org, from the center of power, from people who don't use the tools or feel the friction. If we want to get closer to truth, we have to listen closer to reality. That means involving frontline teams, end users, support staff, and sometimes even the people who are quietly working around the system because it no longer serves them.

Defining value clearly doesn't just help us measure better—it helps us prioritize better. It clarifies trade-offs. It makes disagreements productive. It turns vague goals into design challenges: *If this is what we're trying to improve, what's the simplest thing we can try?* And it helps teams say no with integrity—not to resist, but to stay focused on what matters most.

It also invites transparency. When value is defined, measured, and discussed openly, it becomes a shared language across teams. Product, tech, business, compliance —they stop arguing about *whether* something is valuable and start collaborating on *how* to make it more so. And when things don't work? That's not failure. That's learning. And learning is what transformation actually requires.

So the next time you hear someone say "we need to deliver value," pause. Ask what they mean. Ask who benefits. Ask what would make it obvious that value had been delivered. And ask how we'd know if we were wrong.

Because value isn't a slogan. It's a shared commitment to real improvement. And that starts not with what we say —but with what we choose to measure, what we're willing to question, and what we decide to care about together.

SIMONE SALVO

THE COURAGE TO NOT KNOW
Why letting go of false certainty unlocks real learning

In many transformation efforts, the greatest barrier to progress is not complexity—it's the fear of admitting we don't have all the answers. There's an unspoken expectation in most organizations that leaders should be certain, that teams should have clear plans, and that success is about knowing exactly what to do and how to do it. But in the real world of change, clarity rarely comes upfront. And pretending otherwise does more harm than good.

The truth is, transformation requires us to act before we're fully ready. It asks us to design while we're still discovering, to commit while we're still questioning, and to learn while we build. That's not a flaw—it's a feature. But it only works if we're willing to say the most difficult thing in any high-stakes environment: *we don't know yet*.

This kind of honesty can feel risky. Especially in performance cultures, where ambiguity is mistaken for weakness and questions are seen as delays. Admitting uncertainty is often read as incompetence. So we fake confidence. We build plans that are too neat. We scope work based on assumptions. We promise outcomes we haven't validated. And in doing so, we trade short-term comfort for long-term dysfunction.

The courage to not know isn't about avoiding decisions —it's about making better ones. When we acknowledge what we don't yet understand, we create the space to learn. We test instead of assume. We listen instead of justify. We slow down just enough to see the system more clearly. And often, we discover that what we thought was a problem wasn't the real issue—or that the opportunity was bigger than we imagined.

This shift is especially hard for those used to being right. Subject-matter experts, seasoned leaders, high-performers—they've built their careers on having answers. Letting go of that identity is uncomfortable. But the most impactful transformation leaders I've seen are those who lead with questions. Not because they lack experience, but because they've learned that curiosity travels further than certainty.

Creating a culture where it's safe to not know begins with modeling. When leaders admit what's unclear, others do too. When teams are encouraged to explore without fear of being wrong, ideas get better. When metrics are used to learn rather than to prove, conversations shift from blame to growth. In this way, not knowing becomes a strategic advantage—not a liability.

This doesn't mean endless analysis or decision paralysis. It means learning in motion. Instead of pretending we know, we build small and test early. We ask users what they experience instead of assuming what they want. We try, measure, adapt. We create feedback loops that reward insight, not just output.

It also means changing how we define leadership. Not as the person with the answers, but as the person who creates the conditions for learning. Someone who holds the tension of uncertainty without collapsing into fear or control. Someone who keeps the system moving, even when the path ahead is still emerging.

Transformation work is full of ambiguity. The map is incomplete. The terrain keeps shifting. And the organizations that thrive are not the ones who plan best—but the ones who learn fastest. That learning begins the moment we drop the need to appear certain and pick up the habit of asking better questions.

So ask them. What are we assuming that might not be

true? What do we need to learn before we commit? Who has insight we're not hearing? What's the smallest thing we could try to test this idea?

Because in transformation, progress doesn't come from knowing everything—it comes from knowing what to explore next. And that kind of clarity only arrives when we're brave enough to say, *we don't know… yet.*

DESIGNING FEEDBACK LOOPS THAT WORK
Turning delivery into discovery

One of the most overlooked aspects of digital transformation is feedback—not the kind collected at the end of a project, but the kind designed into the work itself. Most organizations claim to value feedback. They run retrospectives, distribute surveys, hold review meetings. But in practice, feedback often arrives too late, travels too slowly, or gets filtered through too many layers to change anything meaningful. It becomes noise, not signal. Ceremony, not learning.

If we want to move from output to outcome, we need to treat feedback not as an event, but as a system. Something intentionally architected into how we build, deliver, and adapt. Not just to evaluate performance, but to shape it. Not just to measure impact, but to discover what matters. This means designing feedback loops that are fast, honest, and actionable.

The first shift is timing. Most feedback mechanisms are retrospective. We look back at what we did and try to learn from it. But in complex environments, that's often too slow. What we needed to know came much earlier—when the user got confused, when the team misaligned, when the signal first showed up that our assumptions might be wrong. By the time we collect formal feedback, the moment for course correction has passed.

That's why high-functioning teams design for *early feedback*. They create prototypes instead of polished decks. They release slices of functionality instead of waiting for the full feature. They don't just ask users what they think—they observe what users do. The goal is to shrink the distance between action and information. To move from guesswork to grounded insight, before the cost of change gets too high.

The second shift is honesty. Feedback is only useful if it's real. But in many organizations, people are trained to edit themselves. To say what's safe, not what's true. To avoid conflict, preserve harmony, and protect reputations. This makes sense—especially in systems where feedback has been used to punish rather than improve. But it also means that the most valuable insights often go unspoken.

Creating honest feedback loops requires psychological safety. That's not something you get by declaring it—it's something you build by listening without defensiveness, responding with transparency, and acting on what you hear. When people see that their input leads to change, they offer more of it. When they see it ignored, they stop sharing. Feedback, like trust, is reciprocal.

The third shift is actionability. Feedback that can't be acted on is just commentary. For feedback to drive outcomes, it needs to be specific, contextual, and tied to a decision or direction. "This doesn't feel right" might be valid, but "This step breaks the user's flow because of X" is what allows a team to respond. The more you invite feedback tied to observed behavior, not opinion, the more useful it becomes.

This also means giving feedback somewhere to land. If your team has no power to adapt the work, no access to decision-makers, or no room in the process to iterate, then even great feedback dies on arrival. Feedback loops must be connected to autonomy. The ability to learn only matters if you have the permission to respond.

Designing effective feedback loops also challenges how organizations define success. Instead of proving we were right, the goal becomes learning where we were wrong— and doing so as early, cheaply, and kindly as possible. That doesn't mean being negative or skeptical. It means being relentlessly curious. Always asking: what do we know now that we didn't know yesterday? What is the system trying to tell us?

Done right, feedback loops become a source of momentum. Teams adjust in real time. Leaders see risk sooner. Products evolve faster. And the entire system becomes smarter—not because everyone's perfect, but because everyone's learning.

Transformation doesn't stall because people stop working. It stalls because the system stops listening. Feedback is how you keep it alive. Not as a checkbox or a form—but as a habit, a rhythm, and a belief: that the best way to get where we're going is to keep discovering how to get there better.

MAKING OUTCOMES PART OF THE CULTURE
Embedding impact into the way work gets done

Most organizations know how to measure things. Dashboards glow with charts, velocity reports track delivery, and KPIs are updated weekly. There's no shortage of visibility into what's being done. And yet, somewhere in the swirl of tasks completed and features released, something crucial often goes missing: a real connection to the outcome. Not the metric. Not the milestone. The *meaning*.

It's not that people don't care about impact. Quite the opposite. Many teams feel the disconnect acutely. They want their work to matter. They want to see a line between their effort and the change it produces. But when the culture revolves around output—when progress is judged by what moves across a board or gets marked "done"—the outcome becomes abstract. It lives in strategy decks, executive summaries, or quarterly reviews, far removed from the daily pulse of delivery.

This disconnect doesn't show up as a dramatic failure. It shows up quietly. A team launches a new feature, but no one knows if it solved the original problem. A process gets automated, but the inefficiency simply reappears somewhere else. A campaign runs, gets decent numbers, but leaves no lasting impression. Work gets done, but direction feels blurred. Momentum exists, but meaning fades.

The root of the problem isn't measurement. It's mindset. When teams are asked to focus on what they can control—the scope, the sprint, the delivery—they naturally begin to optimize for completion. The faster the delivery, the stronger the signal of productivity. But productivity is not the same as effectiveness. You can ship quickly and still miss the point. You can finish everything and still fail to make a difference.

Bringing outcomes into the center of the culture doesn't mean abandoning delivery. It means redefining what "done" actually means. Not just that the work is complete, but that it had an effect. That something improved. That a real need was met. And that requires a shift—not just in tools or ceremonies, but in how people think about their role.

It starts with questions. Not after the work, but before it. What problem are we trying to solve? For whom? Why now? How will we know if we succeeded? These questions aren't always comfortable. They expose assumptions. They slow things down. But they also create direction. And in cultures that embrace outcomes, those questions aren't considered obstacles—they're considered the work.

Making outcomes cultural means making them visible, not just in the form of metrics, but in conversations. It means teams talking not just about what they're doing, but what they're learning. It means creating space to reflect on whether the thing that was built is actually the thing that was needed. And it means rewarding not just speed or volume, but insight—the kind that sharpens future work.

This isn't a matter of more data. It's a matter of different attention. Listening more closely to users. Observing what changes after a release. Asking what *didn't* happen that we expected. It's about closing the loop not just to celebrate, but to calibrate. Not just to report, but to rethink.

And it's about leadership, too. Leaders shape culture by what they notice, what they question, and what they value. When leaders ask about outcomes, not just progress, they send a signal. When they reward teams for discovering something that challenged the original plan, they create space for truth. When they treat failure as learning and success as shared ownership, they shift the gravitational center from performance to purpose.

In this kind of culture, teams become bolder. Not reckless, but braver in how they explore problems. They look beyond surface-level requests. They take responsibility not just for delivering what was asked, but for understanding what's truly needed. And they become more adaptive—not because they follow the process perfectly, but because they understand what the process is for.

The shift from output to outcome isn't a new framework. It's a new lens. A way of seeing value not just as motion, but as impact. When outcomes become part of the culture, work changes. Meetings become sharper. Decisions become simpler. Focus becomes clearer. And progress becomes real.

Designing for Real Humans

EMPATHY, SYSTEMS THINKING, AND DIGITAL
FRICTION

BEYOND PERSONAS AND PROCESSES
Why real users are messier—and more valuable—than the models

In the world of digital transformation, there's a comforting appeal to neat models. Personas with tidy labels. Journey maps with elegant arcs. Workflows that follow clean arrows from start to finish. We use these tools to make sense of complexity, to align stakeholders, to prioritize features. And they help—up to a point. But eventually, the work of designing for humans runs up against a deeper, messier reality: people don't behave like diagrams.

Real users are inconsistent. They switch contexts. They misinterpret instructions. They multitask, cut corners, and invent workarounds. They care less about your strategy and more about their stress. They don't move linearly through funnels or think in user stories. And the moment we forget this—when we start designing for the artifact instead of the human—we lose the very connection transformation is supposed to create.

This disconnection happens all the time. A beautifully mapped experience gets implemented, only to be ignored. A workflow is digitized, but no one follows it. An app is launched, but usage stalls. The team is confused: we followed the process. We did the research. Why didn't it work?

Because humans don't live in the process. They live in constraints, in habits, in emotions, in noise. And to design for them, we have to be willing to get close. Not just to their behaviors, but to their context. What pressures are they under? What do they believe about their work? What are they solving for that no one has named?

This is where real empathy begins—not as a buzzword, but as a practice. It's not about interviews with pre-written questions. It's about listening for what's unsaid. Watching for the hesitation before a click. Asking follow-ups when the answer sounds rehearsed. And sometimes, it's about observing what people actually do when they don't know they're being observed.

Designing for humans means shifting our orientation. From planning *for* people to building *with* them. From assuming intent to exploring context. From seeking validation to uncovering surprise. It's not always efficient, and it rarely fits neatly into sprint cycles—but it leads to solutions that people actually want to use, because they reflect the reality they inhabit.

This kind of design also challenges our ego. It forces us to let go of the idea that we know best. That our frameworks are correct. That we can optimize the system from the outside. It reminds us that no matter how elegant the architecture, what matters is how it feels to the person inside it.

And it doesn't stop with user experience. Internal tools, team workflows, change programs—these all benefit from human-centered design. When we stop designing *at* people and start designing *with* them, we get better systems, better outcomes, and better relationships. We also get less resistance. Because when people see themselves reflected in a solution—when it solves a problem they actually have—they don't need to be convinced. They lean in.

But this requires a shift in values. Away from abstract efficiency and toward situated utility. Away from best practices and toward lived experience. Away from assuming the user is the problem when things don't work—and toward asking whether the system was designed with the user in mind in the first place.

Personas and processes can be helpful. But they are only tools. The real work is deeper. It's slower. It's messier. And it starts by remembering that humans don't exist to validate our designs. Our designs exist to support their goals. And the more honest we are about that, the more likely we are to create things that don't just function—but matter.

EMBEDDED COMPLEXITY
How real-world constraints shape what people actually do

If you spend enough time observing how people work—really work, not just how they describe it—you start to notice something: almost no one follows the process as designed. Not exactly. They adapt, they bend, they skip steps, they layer their own hacks and rituals over the official flow. This isn't laziness or resistance. It's complexity. And it's always there, hiding in plain sight.

In transformation work, there's often a dangerous assumption that clean design equals good design. We draw the ideal path on a whiteboard, eliminate redundancies, streamline steps, and then wonder why people don't follow it. The answer is rarely that the process is bad. It's that it doesn't account for everything else: competing priorities, legacy systems, emotional labor, incomplete information, interpersonal dynamics, even basic cognitive overload.

People don't operate in isolated flows. They operate in overlapping systems. A customer service rep might be trying to log a complaint while navigating three disconnected platforms, dealing with a frustrated client on the phone, and helping a colleague in real time. An engineer might be updating documentation not because it's useful, but because they know their boss checks version histories. A team might be using a compliance tool not for compliance, but as a proxy for political cover. These are not edge cases—they're normal.

Designing for humans means designing with this embedded complexity in mind. Not trying to eliminate it, but acknowledging it. Making room for it. Instead of building the "right" path and expecting everyone to follow it, we ask: *How does this tool behave when it's not the only thing someone's doing? What happens when priorities conflict? How will someone use this when they're stressed, distracted, or behind schedule?*

These questions lead us to more resilient designs—ones that don't collapse under pressure. They also push us to consider not just the functional aspects of the experience, but the emotional ones. What does this interface communicate under stress? How does it support someone in regaining control, confidence, or clarity? What would it mean for this system to feel *kind*, not just efficient?

This isn't about softening the work. It's about facing its reality. Complexity isn't the enemy of transformation—it's the environment in which it happens. When we ignore it, we end up creating brittle systems, rigid workflows, and tools that break the moment they meet the real world. But when we design with complexity in mind, we create flexibility. We build in slack. We acknowledge that friction will happen—and we plan for it.

One of the most powerful tools for designing with embedded complexity is simply observation. Go where the work happens. Sit with people. Watch what they skip, where they hesitate, what they write on sticky notes or in personal checklists. These behaviors are signals—of what's not working, of what's missing, of where your design has made invisible assumptions.

And then there's language. The way people talk about their work often reveals the dissonance between official systems and lived experience. If people say "I just do it this way because it's faster," that's not resistance—it's insight. If they describe parts of your process as "annoying" or "pointless," they're not being difficult—they're telling you where complexity is unmanaged.

Embedded complexity isn't something to be removed. It's something to be designed through. And when we learn to see it—not as a flaw, but as a feature of human systems

—we start creating things that actually hold up. Not just when the plan is followed, but when real life gets in the way.

That's not a compromise. That's what design for humans actually looks like. Messy. Adaptive. Honest. And ultimately, more successful.

MAKING EMPATHY OPERATIONAL
Why good intentions aren't enough to drive good design

Empathy is a word that gets used a lot in transformation work. It shows up in slide decks, workshops, sticky notes during design sprints. It's praised as the key to understanding users, to building better products, to driving cultural change. But for all the admiration it receives, empathy often remains suspended in the air—conceptual, admired, but untethered. We say it matters. We rarely make it real.

The problem is that empathy sounds soft. It's associated with emotion, with intuition, with slowing down. In environments where velocity and efficiency rule, that can make it feel ornamental. Something you reference to show you care, not something you invest in to improve outcomes. It becomes a word we perform, not a practice we embed.

But empathy isn't about being nice. It's about seeing clearly. It's about recognizing that your assumptions are incomplete, that your vantage point is limited, and that real insight requires humility. When done well, empathy doesn't slow down delivery—it sharpens it. It helps teams focus not just on what people say they want, but on what actually creates value in their context, in their constraints, in their lived reality.

Operationalizing empathy means pulling it down from the abstract and anchoring it in our ways of working. It means treating it not as a one-off activity, but as part of how decisions get made. It starts with asking better questions—not just about what users do, but about how they feel when they do it. Not just what they click, but what they avoid. Not just what they say, but what they don't.

It also means embedding empathy beyond the research

phase. Too often, user understanding is boxed into the early discovery work, then forgotten once building begins. Personas are created, insights captured, but then the project takes on a life of its own. Delivery speeds up. Priorities shift. And the user fades into the background, replaced by features, scope, and deadlines.

Real empathy resists that drift. It stays alive throughout the cycle. It informs not just what we build, but how we test, how we communicate, how we interpret success. It pushes teams to revisit assumptions, to observe without judgment, to reflect on what might have changed. And it invites everyone—not just designers or researchers—to participate in understanding the people they serve.

But embedding empathy is uncomfortable. It introduces friction into the process, the kind that asks, "Are we sure this still makes sense?" or "What might we be missing?" It creates pauses that feel inefficient in the moment but prevent costly missteps later. And it forces teams to sit with ambiguity, to accept that insight rarely arrives in neat, conclusive packages.

Still, the payoff is profound. Products become less about ticking boxes and more about solving problems that matter. Communication becomes clearer, because it's grounded in real language, not just internal jargon. Priorities become more stable, because they're connected to something deeper than internal politics or the latest stakeholder request.

Making empathy operational also requires changing how success is defined. It's not just about usage metrics or delivery velocity—it's about resonance. About whether the things we make truly connect with the people they're made for. And that kind of connection can't be faked. It can't be retrofitted at the end. It has to be designed in from the start, and nurtured along the way.

The teams that do this well aren't necessarily the ones with the best frameworks or the most elegant processes. They're the ones who stay curious. Who listen without rushing to fix. Who let go of being right, in favor of being useful. They ask hard questions not to block progress, but to guide it in the right direction. And they keep returning to the human side of the work—not as a detour, but as the point.

Empathy, when operationalized, stops being a buzz-word. It becomes a discipline. A lens. A quiet force that keeps teams grounded, focused, and honest. It's not about being soft. It's about building things that actually matter.

FRAMING FRICTION AS SIGNAL
Why the things that don't work tell you what really matters

In most organizations, friction is treated like a flaw. When users struggle, when adoption lags, when feedback loops point to confusion, the instinct is to smooth things out. Make the interface cleaner. Shorten the process. Offer more training. And sometimes, these are the right moves. But often, friction isn't just a usability issue—it's a message. A signal. A clue that the system, the workflow, or the decision path is out of sync with real human behavior.

Designing for humans means learning to listen to that friction—not just to eliminate it, but to understand it. Because friction doesn't show up at random. It shows up where needs are unmet, where assumptions don't hold, where tension between different goals has gone unacknowledged. It points us to where the system is misaligned with the people it's meant to serve.

For example, imagine a form that no one completes. Is it too long? Maybe. But maybe it asks for information the user doesn't have—or doesn't trust the organization enough to provide. Maybe the language is vague, or the purpose unclear. Maybe users don't understand what happens after submission. The friction here isn't just about interface—it's about trust, motivation, context.

In transformation work, friction often appears during rollout. Teams hesitate to adopt a new tool. A redesigned workflow gets bypassed. Metrics plateau. Leaders start asking, "Why won't they just use it?" But that's the wrong question. The right question is: *What's the friction telling us about the gap between design and reality?*

That gap might be cultural. People are attached to old systems not because they're perfect, but because they're known. Or it might be emotional—there's anxiety about looking incompetent, fear of judgment, or resentment from not being included in the process. It might even be political—new tools shifting power or visibility in ways that go unspoken.

When we ignore these sources of friction, we miss the deeper design work. We add help text instead of rethinking the flow. We create FAQs instead of addressing the confusion in the first place. We mandate usage instead of redesigning incentives. In doing so, we create systems that look fine on paper, but never truly integrate into how people work and think.

To reframe friction as signal, we have to treat it as data. Not in a statistical sense, but in an ethnographic one. What are people avoiding? Where do they hesitate? When do they rely on workarounds, screenshots, or side conversations to complete a task? These are not signs of failure. They're signs of adaptation—and they tell us what needs to be rethought, not just refined.

This also means being brave enough to dig into complaints. Friction often surfaces first as frustration: "This doesn't make sense." "It takes too long." "It's just easier to do it the old way." These voices are often labeled as resistant or negative. But if you listen carefully, they're often expressing unmet design requirements. They're telling you where your system doesn't fit the real-world complexity of the people using it.

Sometimes, of course, friction comes from change itself. People need time. Familiarity. Confidence. But even in those cases, friction is still useful. It shows you where to focus communication. Where to slow down. Where to invest in training or support. It gives you a map—not of what's broken, but of what matters.

So instead of rushing to remove every bump, pause.

Ask: *What is this moment of friction revealing? What tension is it pointing to? What need is still unmet?* Because if we listen closely, friction stops being something we fix—and starts being something we learn from.

That's the mindset of human-centered design. Not one that eliminates all difficulty, but one that honors it. That sees in every stumble, every detour, every workaround a deeper truth about the people inside the system—and an opportunity to design something better, not just prettier. Something that works not just when everything goes right, but when real life shows up. As it always does.

DESIGNING FOR MOMENTS THAT MATTER
How meaningful experiences are built at the edges, not just the core

Most systems are designed around the average. The expected path. The most common use case. And while that might make sense for efficiency, it often misses where the real emotional weight of experience lives: at the edges. In the awkward moment. The first time. The failure point. The unexpected detour. These are the moments that users remember—not because they happen often, but because when they do, they define how people feel about the system as a whole.

Think about the last time you used a service or product and something went wrong. Could you recover easily? Did it explain itself clearly? Did it treat you with respect, or make you feel small? That moment, whether handled with care or carelessness, likely shaped your trust in the whole system. You might not remember every successful interaction—but you definitely remember the one that broke down.

Designing for humans means paying attention to those moments. The awkward, the anxious, the unclear. The handoff between systems. The empty states. The failure messages. The "we're sorry, something went wrong" screens. Most teams treat these as afterthoughts. But they are where relationships are made—or lost.

The same is true in internal systems. A junior employee submits their first report and doesn't know if it was received. A new hire uses the documentation and finds it outdated. A project manager tries to onboard a stakeholder and gets blocked by permissions. These moments matter—not just because of their task value, but because of what they communicate about how much people matter.

Good human-centered design doesn't just work at the center of the journey. It works at the margins. It's not just about elegant dashboards and seamless transactions. It's about how the system behaves when things don't go as planned. It's about whether people feel seen, supported, and respected—especially when they're confused, frustrated, or unsure.

To design for these moments, teams have to shift their attention. They have to ask different questions: *Where do people feel anxious? Where do they get stuck? What's the first experience like? What happens when something breaks?* They also have to look at real behavior—not just in success flows, but in failure paths, abandoned tasks, and support tickets.

And then they have to *design* for those realities. That means writing microcopy that's not just clear, but kind. It means building feedback loops that close the loop—not just open the channel. It means offering guidance, not just warning. Options, not just dead ends. And sometimes, it means building rituals of support into the system itself—check-ins, reminders, moments of recognition—small signals that show someone was thought about in advance.

These design choices often feel too small to matter in the planning stage. But in practice, they have disproportionate impact. They're the difference between a user who disengages and one who persists. Between an employee who quietly resents a tool and one who recommends it. Between a customer who feels lost and one who feels cared for.

Designing for moments that matter doesn't mean anticipating every possible scenario. It means acknowledging that emotions live in systems too—and designing as if trust is fragile, because it is. When people feel that a system understands not just what they're doing, but *how it feels to do it*, they respond with loyalty, forgiveness, and advocacy. They come back. They invest. They tell others.

Ultimately, human-centered design is not just about making things usable. It's about making them meaningful. And meaning is built, moment by moment—especially in the places where things are hard, not smooth. When we notice those places and build with care, we don't just improve a flow. We build something that matters. Something that earns its place in someone's life, not because it was perfect—but because it was human.

PART III

Making Change Real

HOW TO EXECUTE WITH PURPOSE AND SHIP WHAT MATTERS

In the first two parts of this book, we've examined the invisible forces that hold back change and built the foundational tools and mindsets needed to make transformation possible. But now comes the real work—the execution. This is where ideas are put into motion, where strategies become tangible results, and where all that learning must meet the day-to-day reality of delivering meaningful change.

Making change real is the difference between having a vision and making it happen. It's where ambition and action collide. It's where we stop theorizing about what could be and start creating what *is*. But this is not easy work. In fact, this is where the complexity of transformation becomes most apparent.

Execution requires more than just alignment or resources. It requires focus. It requires prioritization—knowing what to do first and what to leave behind. It requires collaboration across functions and silos, something that is often easier said than done. And it requires constant, honest feedback that can be used to adapt and refine, so that the work stays aligned with its purpose even as circumstances evolve.

In this part of the book, we'll dive into the practicalities of *how* to make change real. We'll explore the art of prioritization—not just in terms of what to deliver, but in terms of what will truly make an impact. We'll look at the critical importance of working across silos, particularly in an era where cross-functional collaboration is the key to unlocking innovation and solving complex problems. And we'll examine the role of feedback loops, ensuring that the change you're making is responsive, adaptable, and ultimately successful in creating lasting impact.

Execution is not just about managing tasks—it's about executing with purpose. It's about making every decision count and ensuring that the changes we implement aren't just noise, but true progress. This is where your ability to translate strategic goals into tactical, actionable steps will define the success of your transformation efforts.

So, as we dig into the mechanics of execution, it's essential to remember that it's not just about speed—it's about meaningful progress. The ideas and principles we'll explore here will help you bridge the gap between vision and reality. With the right focus, collaboration, and feedback, you can ensure that the change you set out to create isn't just a momentary shift, but a lasting transformation.

The Art of Prioritization

THE COST OF A LONG BACKLOG
How unchecked backlogs sap focus and kill momentum

Every transformation effort starts with excitement. Teams are energized. Ideas are flowing. Backlogs begin to grow. New features, enhancements, bug fixes, processes to streamline—the list seems endless, but manageable. The strategy is clear, the vision is in place, and everyone is ready to get to work.

But then something happens. The backlog grows longer. And longer. The focus starts to drift. What seemed like a manageable list becomes a monstrous compilation of "to-dos" that no one knows where to start with. It's easy to fall into the trap of thinking that just because things are moving, we're making progress. But progress without focus is like running in place—you're exerting energy, but you're not going anywhere.

A long, unchecked backlog is one of the most insidious challenges in transformation. It doesn't just slow down delivery—it kills momentum. Teams can't focus on what truly matters. Instead, they're left scrambling to meet deadlines, checking off tasks without ever really stepping back to ask: *What should we be doing right now?* The outcome? Projects get fragmented. Value is diluted. The change we're trying to create remains out of reach.

The first step in addressing a bloated backlog is to accept that not everything needs to be done. In fact, most of it doesn't. This isn't just about managing scope. It's about refining priorities and aligning them with the larger goals of the transformation. But how do you decide what truly matters?

The key is clarity. Without a clear sense of purpose, the backlog becomes a dumping ground for every idea, every request, every shiny object. When leaders and teams fail to define what constitutes real impact, they let the backlog run wild. But when the vision is well-articulated, and the goals are understood, decisions become easier. Focus sharpens. And the transformation becomes a series of strategic moves, not random bursts of activity.

An effective way to approach this is by breaking the backlog down into tiers of priority. What's critical for the transformation to succeed? What's important, but can be deferred? What's nice to have, but won't move the needle? By categorizing tasks and projects based on their contribution to the overall goal, we can bring order to chaos.

And just as importantly, we need to ask: *What will this cost us if we don't do it?* Sometimes, the highest priority item isn't the one with the most obvious payoff. It's the one with the highest risk if left unchecked. Managing a backlog isn't just about delivering features—it's about minimizing risk and making sure the most important things are addressed first.

So, the next time you look at a backlog that feels

unmanageable, stop. Don't just add more tasks. Take the time to sort through it. Cut away the unnecessary. Focus on what drives value. And remind your team that not everything on the list will get done—and that's okay. What matters is that the right things do.

By prioritizing effectively, we create focus. And with focus, we gain momentum—a momentum that propels the transformation forward with purpose and clarity.

ALIGNING STRATEGY WITH DELIVERY
How to bridge the gap between vision and execution

Strategy is often treated as something grand and distant—crafted by senior leadership, shaped in quiet rooms, announced with fanfare. Delivery, by contrast, lives closer to the ground. It's what teams do every day: writing code, solving bugs, making tradeoffs, shipping work. And while both matter, they often exist in parallel worlds. Strategy becomes an idea. Delivery becomes motion. And somewhere between the two, meaning gets lost.

This gap isn't always visible at first. On paper, everything aligns. OKRs link to roadmaps, initiatives map to goals, decks highlight the flow from vision to execution. But the day-to-day tells a different story. Teams are making decisions that feel disconnected from the bigger picture. Priorities shift without explanation. Efforts multiply, but momentum stalls. People work hard, but can't explain how their work fits into anything larger than their backlog.

It's a quiet drift, not a dramatic break. And it often comes from good intentions. Delivery teams want to unblock each other, to keep things moving. Product leads want to respond to feedback, to stay agile. Leaders want to show progress, to demonstrate value. But when those movements happen without a strong anchor to strategy, they scatter. And even when things get done, they don't necessarily move anything forward.

The result is familiar: lots of output, unclear outcomes. Features released without clear use cases. Projects completed that no one really uses. Metrics reported that don't tell us what matters. And behind it all, a growing frustration—not because people don't care, but because they care and feel increasingly disconnected from purpose.

Aligning strategy with delivery isn't about tighter control. It's about clearer conversation. It starts by recognizing that strategy is not a set of instructions, but a set of questions: What are we really trying to achieve? What are we willing to trade off? What does success actually look like—for users, for the business, for the system as a whole?

These questions aren't answered once and forgotten. They need to live inside the delivery process. They need to shape how priorities are discussed, how decisions are made, how uncertainty is handled. Strategy becomes real when it's not just referenced at the start, but revisited throughout. When it becomes a compass, not a document.

That shift requires trust. It means giving teams access to strategic context, not just tasks. It means creating space to challenge priorities—not to slow things down, but to strengthen focus. It means encouraging teams to think, not just execute. And it means recognizing that alignment is dynamic. As reality changes, strategy must adapt—and so must the delivery that follows.

The best teams operate in a loop. They connect the dots between what they're building and why. They bring questions back to leadership when direction is unclear. They share signals from users and systems, helping shape strategy from the ground up. And they understand that prioritization isn't a ranking exercise—it's a strategic act. Every yes is a no to something else. Every decision shapes direction.

None of this is easy. It takes time, discipline, and a shared language. It requires leaders to be transparent about the "why," not just the "what." It asks teams to think critically, not just move quickly. But when it works, the impact is profound. Delivery becomes more than motion—it becomes progress. And strategy becomes more than intent—it becomes reality.

Alignment isn't a state you reach. It's a practice you maintain. Not with templates or rituals, but with ongoing clarity, conversation, and care. That's how you turn ambition into action. That's how you make strategy visible in every line of code, every story, every outcome that actually matters.

NAVIGATING THE CROSS-FUNCTIONAL COMPLEXITY
How to break down silos and build collaborative momentum

Cross-functional collaboration sounds like a simple idea. Bring people together from different departments, combine their expertise, and solve problems in a more holistic way. On paper, it promises better products, faster learning, and fewer blind spots. But in practice, it rarely feels that smooth. What's meant to be a strength often turns into a source of tension, misunderstanding, and delays.

The challenge doesn't come from bad intent. Most people want to collaborate. They want to build something that works beyond their own scope. But the reality is that every function brings its own language, incentives, and mental models. What feels like clarity to one team can feel like confusion to another. What seems urgent in one area might seem irrelevant in another. And without a shared rhythm, even basic decisions turn into long negotiations.

It often starts subtly. A product manager outlines a roadmap, assuming it's aligned with business priorities. The designers begin sketching, interpreting the goals through the lens of user experience. Meanwhile, engineers look at the same plan and flag technical constraints no one else had considered. Legal raises concerns. Marketing asks for messaging changes. Suddenly, what felt like momentum turns into a maze. Everyone is moving—but not necessarily in the same direction.

The friction is rarely about the work itself. It's about what the work represents. For the business team, a new feature is a market differentiator. For engineers, it's a question of scalability. For designers, it's about usability. For compliance, it's risk exposure. Each perspective is valid.

Each comes with its own logic. And in cross-functional settings, these logics collide—not because anyone's wrong, but because they're looking at different parts of the same system.

Trying to resolve this by forcing consensus rarely works. Endless meetings, alignment sessions, or top-down decisions often create more frustration than clarity. The real breakthrough comes when teams stop trying to simplify the complexity—and start navigating it together.

That means accepting that tension is part of the process. Not something to eliminate, but something to work through. It means building relationships that go beyond roles. Taking the time to understand not just what another team needs, but how they think, what they value, where their constraints live. It means asking real questions, not just waiting for your turn to speak. And it means showing up not as a representative of your function, but as a partner in a shared outcome.

The teams that navigate this complexity well don't eliminate silos. They create bridges. They invest in trust before it's needed. They normalize disagreement without making it personal. They let go of the fantasy that everyone will naturally align, and instead, create systems where alignment is actively built. Not just through structure, but through culture.

And that culture isn't about being nice. It's about being real. Saying when things don't make sense. Surfacing trade-offs early. Being transparent about what's known, what's assumed, and what's uncertain. It's about leaving space for nuance—because in cross-functional work, the answer is rarely simple. It's often a dance between competing truths, and progress depends on how well you can hold that tension.

When cross-functional complexity is embraced, something powerful happens. Decisions become more robust. Risks get spotted earlier. Products work better not just in theory, but in the messy reality of launch and adoption. And perhaps most importantly, people feel like they're part of something larger than their function. They stop guarding turf and start building together.

Collaboration across silos isn't a matter of structure— it's a matter of posture. A willingness to see the full picture, even when it complicates your part of it. A commitment to building something coherent, not just completing your piece. And a shared belief that complexity isn't the enemy —it's the raw material of meaningful work.

BUILDING A CULTURE OF FEEDBACK
Turning adaptation into action through real-time insights

Feedback is the pulse of any transformation effort. Without it, you risk moving in the wrong direction for far too long. You'll execute based on assumptions, missing opportunities for refinement until it's too late. The more feedback you gather—and the more effectively you respond to it—the more likely you are to adapt, improve, and succeed. But this is easier said than done.

In many organizations, feedback is treated as a periodic event. We gather it through surveys or meetings, then wait for the next cycle. Feedback loops are often seen as something "nice to have," rather than an essential, ongoing practice. The problem with this approach is that the landscape of change is constantly shifting, and if feedback is only collected after major milestones or at set intervals, it's already outdated by the time it's acted upon.

To truly embed feedback into the execution process, it has to be continuous and real-time. This requires designing feedback loops that are woven into every phase of a project. Teams should be actively gathering input as they move through each stage, not just after they've completed something. By the time the project is done, you should have already adapted and improved the solution multiple times based on user insights.

Real-time feedback allows you to catch issues early, often before they even become problems. If something isn't working, you don't wait until the launch phase to find out—you know during development. You can then adjust the course before it's too costly, rather than scrambling to fix a misstep after the fact. This constant adaptation is a hallmark of high-performing teams, especially in environments that prioritize agility and user-centric design.

It's also crucial that feedback is actionable. Gathering data is useless unless you can turn it into insight and, ultimately, action. Teams need to be equipped to interpret feedback effectively, understand its implications, and implement changes quickly. This means not only having the right systems and processes in place but also fostering a mindset where feedback is seen as an essential part of problem-solving.

One of the most important shifts here is moving beyond traditional feedback mechanisms. Instead of relying only on surveys or focus groups, consider observational feedback, user testing, and even informal check-ins. Listening to your team members, stakeholders, and end-users regularly and with genuine curiosity will uncover deeper insights that quantitative data often misses. These are the moments when you can catch frustration, confusion, or delight that will never show up in a standard survey, but that can make or break the success of your transformation.

Feedback is also about creating a culture of openness. Too often, feedback is seen as a critique rather than an opportunity for growth. Teams become defensive, and individuals become reluctant to speak up. To prevent this, create an environment where feedback is normalized, celebrated, and used as a learning tool. Encourage people to share both successes and failures, and make sure everyone feels comfortable giving and receiving feedback. This openness will strengthen collaboration, boost morale, and foster continuous improvement across the board.

Finally, closing the loop is just as important as gathering feedback in the first place. It's easy to ask for feedback, but it's a powerful action to show that you're listening and responding to it. When teams take the time to address concerns or acknowledge feedback in tangible ways, it reinforces trust. People are more likely to continue offering valuable insights when they see that their feedback is valued and acted upon.

Real-time feedback isn't a luxury—it's a competitive necessity. It ensures that you're not making decisions based on outdated information, that you're not missing blind spots, and that you're continuously refining your processes and products. It accelerates the learning curve of your transformation, turning every insight into an opportunity for improvement. By building a culture of feedback into the fabric of your work, you ensure that your transformation is not just implemented but iteratively refined to meet real-world needs and challenges.

CREATING LASTING IMPACT THROUGH CONSISTENCY
How small, steady actions drive big, sustainable change

In the pursuit of transformation, it's easy to get caught up in the desire for rapid, visible results. We want quick wins, fast deliverables, and immediate validation. But while these short-term achievements are valuable for building momentum, they often don't sustain themselves in the long term. True transformation requires more than just bursts of effort. It requires consistency—small, incremental actions taken over time that, when combined, lead to significant and sustainable change.

The challenge of transformation is that it often involves introducing new behaviors, mindsets, and habits into a system that has been operating a certain way for years, if not decades. Changing the course of an organization isn't about flipping a switch. It's about making steady progress that sticks. This is where consistency becomes the bedrock of your transformation journey.

First, let's talk about what consistency looks like. It's about building new routines—things that people can rely on as part of their everyday work. This isn't just about setting new expectations; it's about integrating those expectations into the daily operations of your organization. For instance, regular check-ins or feedback loops should become standard practice. They should be built into the system, so teams don't have to remember to do them—they just happen. These practices create a rhythm and cadence that can help the organization stay on track even when things get chaotic.

Another form of consistency involves reinforcing core values. Transformation is, at its heart, a shift in how we think and act. But values are only truly embedded when they're consistently modeled and reinforced through behavior. Leaders must not only talk about these values—they must live them. It's about showing up consistently, making decisions that align with the transformation goals, and holding others accountable to the same standards. When these behaviors become a part of the organizational fabric, they're no longer seen as 'new' but as integral to the way business is done.

But the challenge with consistency isn't just about doing the same things over and over—it's about doing them with purpose and adaptability. This is why consistency should never be confused with stagnation. If you keep doing the same thing over and over without assessing the outcomes, you're just repeating ineffective actions. To be truly effective, consistency requires periodic reflection and adjustment. It's about maintaining the rhythm of transformation while being flexible enough to adapt when needed.

Measurement is also critical for ensuring consistency leads to results. Regularly tracking progress allows you to see if your actions are moving you closer to your objectives. You need to be looking not just at outputs but at outcomes—whether those incremental steps are contributing to the larger vision. If something's not working, consistent measurement allows you to course-correct early. But if you're not measuring consistently, it's easy to drift off course without realizing it.

In the context of transformation, consistency also means keeping the momentum going when the initial enthusiasm begins to fade. The first few months of a transformation effort are often energized by novelty and excitement. But as time goes on, the pace can slow, distractions increase, and priorities shift. This is when leadership must step in to reignite the fire. Leaders need to ensure that the urgency of the transformation doesn't dissipate. They must continue to advocate for it, model the behaviors, and celebrate the small wins along the way to remind everyone that transformation is ongoing.

Finally, consistency is about building a long-term vision that transcends any single project, product, or initiative. Transformation isn't about one-and-done efforts—it's about shaping the organization for the future. It's about creating systems, habits, and practices that will sustain change long after the transformation initiative has ended. By embedding transformation into the DNA of the organization, leaders ensure that change doesn't just happen in bursts but is woven into the fabric of how the company operates.

The key to transformation is not doing big things—it's about doing the right things, consistently. Transformation is a marathon, not a sprint. And to finish it, you need the endurance to keep going, even when the finish line isn't in sight. It's about building steady, sustainable momentum through daily actions, measurement, and reflection. When you approach transformation with this mindset, you're not just driving change—you're shaping a culture that can continue to evolve, adapt, and thrive.

Working Across Silos

COLLABORATION TACTICS FOR CROSS-FUNCTIONAL
SUCCESS

THE COST OF SILOS
How disconnection slows down progress and innovation

Silos are often a silent but powerful force that holds organizations back from true transformation. They're the invisible walls that separate teams, departments, and even leadership from each other, creating a divide that hampers communication, innovation, and the flow of ideas. Each team, isolated within its own function, operates in its own bubble. While this might seem efficient at first, it's a dangerous illusion.

When teams work in silos, they lose sight of the bigger picture. Each group optimizes for its own success without understanding how its efforts fit into the larger organizational goals. This disconnection leads to duplication of work, missed opportunities, and slower decision-making. For example, a product development team may create a feature based on its own insights, only to find that marketing is preparing a campaign for something entirely different, or that the sales team hasn't been briefed on the feature's value. The result is confusion, inefficiency, and missed chances for delivering value to customers.

The most critical cost of silos, however, is innovation. Innovation thrives on collaboration—on the sharing of diverse ideas and perspectives. When teams are isolated, innovation is stifled. The lack of collaboration leads to narrow thinking and unoriginal solutions. Without input from other functions, product development teams may miss important user needs. Marketing may fail to understand what drives product value. And leadership may struggle to see how different initiatives are interrelated.

But the problem with silos goes beyond the obvious inefficiencies. It's also about the impact on culture. When teams work in isolation, trust erodes. People stop seeing each other as partners in success and start seeing each other as obstacles or competitors. The workplace becomes fragmented. Without a cohesive, shared vision, teams can become territorial, defending their own space rather than working toward a common goal.

The impact on productivity is clear: teams are slower to act, more likely to make mistakes, and less effective at implementing change. Cross-functional projects stall. Deadlines slip. The organization becomes reactive rather than proactive.

Overcoming silos isn't just about organizing differently. It's about changing the mindset. It's about fostering a culture where collaboration isn't an afterthought, but a core principle. This means not just bringing teams together physically, but aligning them toward shared objectives, open communication, and a collective commitment to success.

The challenge, then, is how to break down these barriers. How do you build bridges between departments that have traditionally worked in isolation? How do you foster a culture of collaboration in an organization where silos have been in place for years?

It starts with intentionality. Building the right structures, tools, and processes to encourage collaboration is essential. But perhaps more importantly, it requires leadership that actively works to dismantle the barriers. Leaders must set the tone by modeling collaboration and emphasizing shared goals over individual success. They must ensure that teams understand the importance of cross-functional work and provide the support needed to make it happen.

In the end, breaking down silos is not about changing the organizational chart—it's about changing the way people think and work together. When teams collaborate seamlessly, they can move faster, create better solutions, and respond more effectively to the ever-changing needs of the business and its customers. The true power of an organization is realized when the walls between teams come down, and all functions are aligned toward a common vision of success.

That's the essence of working across silos: collaboration isn't just nice to have—it's essential for progress. Without it, innovation is limited, productivity is undermined, and transformation is stalled. So how do we make collaboration work? Let's explore the tools and strategies that enable cross-functional success.

BREAKING DOWN BARRIERS WITH INTENTIONAL STRUCTURES
How to design processes and environments that promote cross-functional collaboration

To overcome silos, simply telling teams to "work together" is rarely effective. Collaboration doesn't happen on its own —it requires intentional, strategic effort. Organizational structures, processes, and environments must be carefully designed to encourage interaction, communication, and a shared sense of purpose. Without these elements, collaboration becomes an abstract idea, not a functional reality.

One of the first steps in promoting collaboration is to design cross-functional teams that can tackle complex problems holistically. These teams should include members from different functions—product, engineering, marketing, sales, customer support—who bring diverse perspectives and expertise to the table. Rather than working in isolation on their respective tasks, team members should have a common goal that they collaborate on achieving together.

Creating these teams requires a shift in how we think about roles and responsibilities. For instance, instead of relying on separate "silos" of work where each department holds exclusive ownership over their area, consider assigning ownership of problems or projects to a team as a whole. These cross-functional teams should have the authority to make decisions that influence the direction of the project, allowing them to move faster and more decisively. By placing power in the hands of the teams, you eliminate delays caused by waiting for approval from different parts of the organization.

Next, processes need to be designed to facilitate collaboration, not hinder it. This starts with aligning workflows. It's important that teams working on the same projects have shared timelines, milestones, and goals. This may require adopting collaborative project management tools that provide visibility across departments, ensuring that all team members are on the same page. Tools like Jira, Trello, or Asana can help provide transparency and ensure that progress is tracked in real time, reducing the chances of miscommunication and bottlenecks.

Having clear meeting cadences is another key element. Regular check-ins across departments ensure that teams are aligned on their progress and challenges. These meetings can be daily or weekly, depending on the pace of the project. However, simply having regular meetings isn't enough—it's important that these meetings are designed with purpose. They should be structured to encourage collaboration, discussion, and problem-solving, not just status updates. This creates a forum where issues can be raised, and solutions can be co-created.

Additionally, creating physical or virtual spaces where people from different departments can meet informally can encourage spontaneous collaboration. Whether it's through open-plan offices or virtual channels like Slack or Microsoft Teams, informal interactions often lead to new ideas and solutions that wouldn't arise in a formal meeting. Encouraging teams to interact on a personal level, even for short bursts during the day, can break down mental and emotional barriers and help foster a collaborative mindset.

Shared goals are also essential for successful cross-functional collaboration. Each team must understand how their individual contributions fit into the larger picture. Leaders must make it clear how each department's work feeds into the broader strategic objectives of the organization. This shared understanding of the mission will help remove the "us vs. them" mentality that often arises when silos are present.

In order to keep teams motivated, recognition and reward systems must be designed to celebrate cross-functional collaboration. Instead of rewarding teams based solely on departmental KPIs, recognize those that work together across functions to drive broader organizational success. This can take the form of awards, public acknowledgment, or incentives. When teams see that collaboration is valued and rewarded, they are more likely to engage in it.

Creating an environment conducive to collaboration is a gradual process. It requires intentional structuring of teams, workflows, processes, and incentives. But when done correctly, the results are far-reaching. A well-designed system encourages departments to work together efficiently, drives innovation, and accelerates the pace of change. By breaking down the barriers between silos, organizations can create a more cohesive, agile, and successful workforce. The foundation of collaboration is built on the understanding that no one department has all the answers—and that the most effective solutions arise when diverse minds come together.

CULTIVATING A COLLABORATIVE MINDSET
How to shift from individual success to collective achievement

While structures, processes, and tools are vital in enabling cross-functional collaboration, they are only part of the equation. For collaboration to truly thrive, it needs to be underpinned by a collaborative mindset—a shift in how people approach their work and how they perceive their role within the broader organization. Without this mindset, even the best systems and tools can fall flat.

In traditional work environments, there is often a strong emphasis on individual achievement. Employees are measured based on their ability to meet their own goals, hit their own targets, and complete their individual tasks. While this is important, it doesn't always align with the needs of today's fast-moving, complex organizations. In the face of major transformation, collaboration becomes essential for success, and the ability to work well with others becomes more important than personal accomplishment.

The first step in shifting to a collaborative mindset is to redefine success. Instead of focusing solely on individual KPIs or departmental goals, success should be framed as the achievement of shared objectives. It's about recognizing that the work of one team is interdependent with the work of others, and that the greatest value comes when everyone works together to solve problems and create solutions.

To build this mindset, leaders need to encourage inter-departmental dialogue. Teams must understand the objectives, challenges, and limitations of other teams. Cross-functional meetings and activities where team members from different departments come together to discuss common challenges, exchange insights, and offer solutions are essential. When people from different backgrounds and expertise come together, they are more likely to see things from different perspectives, which can lead to more creative and effective problem-solving.

Additionally, leaders should model the behavior they want to see in their teams. If leaders consistently prioritize collaboration and teamwork, they set the tone for the rest of the organization. Leaders should be transparent about their own struggles, seek input from others, and emphasize the importance of collective achievement. By doing this, they demonstrate that no one person or team has all the answers—and that the ability to work well with others is just as important as technical expertise.

Another key to fostering a collaborative mindset is the empowerment of individuals. When people feel like they have a voice in the decision-making process and are given the freedom to contribute to projects across functions, they're more likely to feel invested in the outcome. This doesn't mean giving up individual responsibility—it means encouraging individuals to take ownership not just of their own work, but also of the collective effort. Empowerment can come in the form of responsibility for cross-functional projects, influence over decision-making, or being part of collaborative teams where input is valued and acted upon.

Trust is also a fundamental element in cultivating a collaborative mindset. Without trust, collaboration becomes difficult, as team members may be hesitant to share ideas or give feedback. Building trust takes time and requires intentional effort. It's about creating an environment where team members feel safe to speak openly, make mistakes, and learn from each other. Trust is fostered when leaders create an atmosphere of psychological safety, where

125

people feel valued not just for what they achieve but for how they contribute to the team.

At the heart of collaboration is the recognition that every team member brings unique skills, perspectives, and experiences to the table. Collaboration works best when it taps into the diversity of thought—when people are encouraged to challenge assumptions, bring new ideas, and leverage their own strengths in solving complex problems. But in order for this to happen, team members must respect one another's contributions and work toward mutual understanding. This can sometimes be difficult, especially in organizations where silos have been entrenched for years, but it is essential for long-term success.

Another powerful tool for cultivating a collaborative mindset is celebrating collective achievements. When teams reach milestones or complete projects, the focus should be on celebrating the collective effort, not just individual success. Recognition can come in many forms, from public acknowledgments to team outings or simple thank-yous. By emphasizing the importance of collaboration in achieving goals, leaders can inspire the organization to work together in pursuit of common objectives.

CREATING STRUCTURES THAT SUPPORT COLLABORATION
Designing workflows, tools, and systems that promote effective teamwork

Creating a culture of collaboration is essential, but it must be supported by the right structures, processes, and tools. In many organizations, good intentions for collaboration falter due to a lack of proper systems that facilitate cross-functional work. Without the right infrastructure in place, teams fall back into silos, relying on outdated workflows and inefficient communication methods.

The first step in creating structures that support collaboration is streamlining communication channels. In silos, communication tends to be isolated—each department communicates only within its own boundaries. To overcome this, organizations need to establish communication practices that allow teams from different departments to interact regularly, share updates, and address challenges. This can be achieved by using collaborative platforms like Slack, Microsoft Teams, or Google Workspace, which allow teams to create shared channels where they can communicate in real-time. This ensures that everyone stays aligned and can easily share insights or request assistance from other departments.

Alongside communication tools, project management tools are essential for keeping cross-functional teams organized. Tools like Trello, Asana, Jira, or Monday.com enable teams to track the progress of shared initiatives in real-time. By using a centralized project management tool, teams can see what tasks are being worked on, who is responsible for what, and how everything fits into the larger project. This transparency eliminates confusion and keeps everyone on the same page, reducing the chances of tasks falling through the cracks.

In addition to communication and project management tools, shared documentation systems are key. When teams collaborate, it's essential that everyone has access to the same information. Tools like Confluence, Notion, or Google Docs allow multiple team members to contribute to documents, share notes, and update key resources. With shared documentation, teams can reference the same set of information, ensuring consistency and minimizing miscommunication. Furthermore, maintaining clear, updated documentation helps new team members get up to speed quickly, without having to sift through siloed knowledge.

Cross-functional meetings should also be part of the structural design. These meetings ensure that all teams are kept informed and aligned. However, simply having a meeting is not enough. Meetings must be structured and purposeful, focusing on problem-solving and decision-making rather than status updates. One effective way to organize cross-functional meetings is to adopt a meeting cadence that allows different teams to come together regularly to discuss progress, challenges, and opportunities. This cadence can vary depending on the project but should be frequent enough to keep momentum without becoming a drain on team productivity.

Another vital structure is clear ownership of cross-functional initiatives. In many cases, projects stall because no one takes ultimate responsibility for driving them forward. Cross-functional projects often involve many stakeholders, and without someone to coordinate efforts, things can easily become disjointed. Assigning a project manager or leader who is responsible for the overall initiative ensures that there is someone who keeps everything on track. This person acts as a bridge, ensuring that all team members have what they need and that the project stays aligned with its strategic goals.

A structure that also encourages collaboration is cross-functional training. It's often easy for people to stay within their department's expertise and ways of working. To break down barriers, organizations can offer training that helps employees understand the roles and challenges of other departments. For example, product teams can learn about marketing strategies, marketing teams can learn about product development processes, and operations teams can understand customer service challenges. By giving employees a broad understanding of different func-tions, they are more likely to approach cross-functional collaboration with empathy and a better understanding of the interdependencies between teams.

BUILDING TRUST ACROSS FUNCTIONS
The foundation of collaboration: How to create a safe environment for cross-functional work

No matter how carefully you design processes or choose tools, collaboration will always fail without trust. Trust is the most essential ingredient in successful teamwork, and it is often the thing that's hardest to cultivate—especially across functions. When teams work in silos for extended periods, trust breaks down. People become skeptical of others' motives or work, and communication suffers as a result. But collaboration is only possible when teams trust each other to deliver on promises, share vital information, and respect differing viewpoints.

Building trust across functions begins with vulnerability. Leaders must model openness and willingness to share both successes and challenges. They should encourage transparency about what is working and what isn't, as well as the context around certain decisions. When teams see that leadership is willing to be open about the struggles and uncertainties of transformation, they are more likely to replicate that behavior within their own teams. This openness sets a tone that makes collaboration easier, as it encourages people to express concerns or ask for help without fear of judgment.

Another way to build trust is through shared goals. When teams clearly understand that they are working toward the same objectives, it fosters a sense of unity. Trust grows when people feel like they are all pulling in the same direction. A shared vision ensures that everyone is aligned, which makes it easier for team members to believe that their colleagues are invested in the same outcomes. It also creates a sense of accountability—if one team falters, it affects everyone. The common pursuit of success binds the team, making collaboration feel less like a series of individual tasks and more like a group effort.

Setting expectations is also critical in fostering trust. If team members are unsure of what's expected of them, they may hold back or, worse, misunderstand their role in the collaborative process. Establishing clear, transparent expectations upfront allows team members to operate with confidence. For example, defining who is responsible for what, how often meetings will occur, and how decisions will be made, creates a structure within which trust can grow. When people know what to expect from each other, it eliminates unnecessary friction and miscommunication.

In cross-functional teams, trust is also built by recognizing expertise. Each team brings a unique set of skills, and it's vital that everyone in the group respects and acknowledges what each function contributes. In some cases, departments may be skeptical of other teams' skills or priorities, especially when they haven't had much previous interaction. To overcome this, leaders should foster an appreciation for diversity of thought and expertise. They should remind teams that their collective strength lies in combining different perspectives. Respecting others' contributions, regardless of their department, is a foundational element of trust-building.

Listening actively is another key practice in building trust. It's easy to listen just enough to respond, but true listening requires active engagement. When people feel heard, they feel valued, and this trust can lead to more open and productive collaboration. Actively listening means not only hearing the words being said but understanding the emotions, concerns, and motivations behind them. By giving colleagues the space to voice their opinions without interruption, leaders show that they are willing to invest time in understanding differing points of view.

Celebrating successes together is an important part of building trust. When teams achieve a goal, no matter how small, it's crucial that everyone celebrates together. Acknowledging contributions from all functions demonstrates that trust has been earned and reinforces the sense of a shared mission. A simple "thank you" or public recognition can go a long way in strengthening relationships. Recognizing collaborative success, whether through verbal praise, rewards, or shared celebrations, lets everyone know that their contribution matters and that trust has led to collective achievement.

Building trust is an ongoing process. It requires consistent effort, patience, and a focus on relationships. Trust is easily lost but hard-won, which is why it needs to be actively cultivated over time. However, the payoff is immense. Teams that trust one another communicate more effectively, work more efficiently, and feel more motivated to contribute to the success of the organization. Trust becomes the cornerstone of high-performing, cross-functional teams—teams that drive change, overcome challenges, and create meaningful outcomes together. Without it, collaboration remains an ideal rather than a reality. But when trust is in place, collaboration becomes an unstoppable force, enabling the organization to move toward its transformation goals with unity and purpose.

Feedback Loops That Work

THE POWER OF REAL-TIME FEEDBACK
Why feedback is the key to continuous improvement, not just a check-in

In a world where everything is constantly evolving, from technology to customer needs, relying on outdated feedback mechanisms is no longer enough. The traditional model of waiting for the end of a project to gather feedback is no longer viable in the fast-paced, competitive landscape of today. Instead, real-time feedback has become an essential tool for continuous improvement and innovation.

The power of real-time feedback lies in its immediacy and relevance. When feedback is provided as events are unfolding, teams can make instant adjustments to their processes, products, and strategies. In traditional project management models, feedback would come after a project had been completed, making it difficult, if not impossible, to make any necessary changes without starting from scratch. With real-time feedback, problems can be identified early and solved before they become insurmountable issues. This allows teams to move faster, improve constantly, and stay agile.

Real-time feedback also ensures that the feedback provided is directly relevant to the work at hand. It's not a general review of a project completed months ago; it's a live commentary on ongoing work, helping teams understand exactly how their actions are contributing to the project's success or failure. For example, when user feedback is collected immediately after an interaction with a product or service, the information is still fresh, enabling teams to act on it quickly.

However, to truly capitalize on real-time feedback, it must be actionable. Feedback that is vague or nonspecific won't help teams improve. The goal of collecting feedback in real-time is to provide insights that can be directly translated into actionable steps. This means the feedback must be clear, specific, and focused on areas where improvements can be made immediately. For instance, rather than saying, "This feature isn't great," actionable feedback might say, "The navigation button is hard to find; it needs to be bigger or relocated." This level of detail gives the team specific guidance on what to address.

Additionally, real-time feedback is not just about gathering information—it's also about creating a culture of continuous improvement. When feedback is integrated into daily workflows, it fosters an environment where learning becomes a part of the process, rather than an afterthought. In traditional models, feedback would be gathered at the end of a project, often too late to make meaningful changes. Real-time feedback, however, allows teams to iterate and improve continuously, which is crucial for long-term success. It enables teams to experiment, take risks, and learn from each iteration, making it a vital component of any modern organizational strategy.

Real-time feedback is also crucial for agility. The traditional project management models, especially those used in waterfall methodologies, follow rigid steps and timelines. Feedback often comes at the end, after a product is completed or a milestone is reached. This doesn't leave much room for adaptation or changes along the way. On the other hand, agile teams rely on real-time feedback to adjust their work processes and outputs as they go. This feedback is a core part of what makes agile so effective— teams are able to pivot quickly when things aren't working and adjust their direction to better meet the needs of the project.

An essential aspect of real-time feedback is that it encourages collaboration. When feedback is delivered in real time, it's not just a top-down critique or a formal report; it's an opportunity for team members, customers, or stakeholders to interact with each other and share their perspectives. This collaborative nature of feedback helps to break down silos, encourage open communication, and promote teamwork. Teams are more likely to share insights, ask questions, and propose solutions when they know their feedback will be heard and acted upon quickly.

However, for real-time feedback to be truly effective, it must be integrated into existing workflows and tools. It's not enough to simply ask for feedback—it needs to be part of the day-to-day process. Teams should have the tools and systems in place to easily gather feedback from customers, stakeholders, or team members, whether through surveys, meetings, or digital platforms. These systems should allow for seamless communication, making it easy to track, evaluate, and respond to feedback in real-time. Without these systems in place, the process of collecting and using feedback can quickly become disjointed and inefficient.

It's important to measure the impact of the feedback

received. Real-time feedback is only valuable if it leads to real change. Teams should track how they use feedback to improve their products or processes and measure the results of those changes. Are customer complaints decreasing? Are teams achieving better results with less effort? By measuring the impact of feedback, organizations can better understand its effectiveness and make adjustments to their feedback systems as needed.

Real-time feedback is a game-changer for organizations looking to stay competitive and innovative. By gathering feedback as events unfold, teams can make immediate adjustments, solve problems quickly, and maintain momentum. However, real-time feedback is only effective when it's clear, actionable, and integrated into the organization's daily workflow. By fostering a culture of continuous improvement, collaboration, and agility, real-time feedback can drive success and help organizations thrive in an ever-changing world.

AVOIDING THE "FAKE AGILE" TRAP
How to ensure feedback isn't just a checkbox activity

Many organizations claim to practice Agile methodologies, but too often, they fall into the trap of the "Fake Agile" mindset. In these environments, feedback is treated as a formality, a simple box to check off in a process, rather than as a genuine, ongoing effort to improve and iterate. This kind of superficial approach can undermine the true potential of Agile practices and limit the benefits of continuous feedback loops.

The core of genuine Agile feedback is the recognition that it is not a one-time event or an isolated activity. It should be part of an ongoing dialogue, where the insights gathered from each iteration, sprint, or product launch are used to improve future work. The problem arises when organizations use feedback sessions as a ritualistic exercise—they gather feedback, maybe hold a retrospective or two, and then move on to the next phase without actually acting on what was said. This doesn't lead to progress—it leads to stagnation.

To avoid falling into the "Fake Agile" trap, feedback must be actionable. Simply gathering feedback without planning how to use it can create a false sense of progress. Teams may feel they are making changes or improving, but if feedback isn't actually being integrated into the process, it's just a symbolic act, not a valuable tool. The feedback should inform concrete actions. For instance, if the team identifies a gap in user experience, they should not just acknowledge it; they must prioritize it, assign responsibility for improvement, and track progress in real time.

A key element to making feedback actionable is clear ownership. In many organizations, feedback can become too diffuse or unstructured. The feedback gathered from retrospectives or reviews often goes into a list of suggestions with no clear accountability. Without someone being responsible for acting on the feedback, nothing will get done. Whether it's a product manager, a team lead, or even a cross-functional group, someone needs to be designated to own the feedback and ensure that it leads to real, measurable changes. This ownership helps prevent feedback from getting lost in the shuffle or reduced to mere lip service.

Additionally, feedback should be tracked and revisited. Many organizations make the mistake of gathering feedback and then moving forward without reflecting on how the actions based on that feedback have played out. If feedback from one sprint identified issues with a particular feature, teams should revisit those issues in subsequent reviews to assess if the improvements were effective or if further adjustments are necessary. Tracking feedback is about creating a feedback loop where changes are evaluated, tested, and refined over time. This process ensures that feedback is not a one-off activity but a living process that shapes the ongoing development of the product or project.

Another way to avoid the "Fake Agile" trap is to embed feedback into the daily workflow. It should not be reserved for specific meetings or retrospectives, but rather integrated into day-to-day tasks. For instance, teams can gather real-time feedback during customer interactions, use analytics to continuously monitor product performance, or conduct brief daily check-ins to address small issues before they become bigger problems. The more frequently feedback is gathered and acted upon, the more responsive and agile the team becomes. Daily or even hourly feedback loops can help teams stay aligned and make improvements in real time, rather than waiting for the next sprint to catch up with issues that have already compounded.

Feedback should also be aligned with key objectives. Often, feedback gathered in Agile teams can feel disjointed or unfocused, with people offering feedback on minor issues that don't necessarily align with the overall goals of the project. It's important to ensure that feedback aligns with the core business objectives and user needs. This requires prioritizing feedback that impacts the most important aspects of the project, such as critical features, customer satisfaction, or system performance. Feedback should be relevant to the project's overall success and tied directly to measurable outcomes.

Making feedback part of the organizational culture is essential to avoiding the "Fake Agile" trap. In many cases, feedback is treated as something temporary—something that only matters for the duration of a sprint or project. However, organizations that genuinely embrace Agile understand that feedback is a core value that should inform all aspects of the business, from product development to customer service, to leadership and decision-making. This requires leadership buy-in and creating an environment where feedback is encouraged and appreciated at all levels of the organization. When feedback becomes part of the culture, it's not just a checkbox activity —it's an integral part of how the organization evolves and grows.

Avoiding the "Fake Agile" trap requires a shift in mindset from feedback as a formality to feedback as an actionable tool for continuous improvement. By ensuring that feedback is specific, actionable, tracked, and aligned with the organization's goals, teams can avoid the pitfalls of superficial feedback and use it to drive meaningful change. The true power of Agile lies in its ability to help organizations adapt, evolve, and continuously improve, and that power is unlocked only when feedback is treated as an essential, ongoing process that informs every decision and action. By embedding feedback into the daily work-flow and making it a cultural norm, organizations can build an environment that is truly agile—one that thrives on continuous improvement and adapts swiftly to new challenges and opportunities.

CREATING A FEEDBACK CULTURE
How to embed continuous feedback in your organization's DNA

Building a true feedback culture within an organization is not a quick fix—it's a long-term commitment that involves everyone, from leadership to individual team members. For feedback to work effectively, it cannot be relegated to quarterly reviews or sporadic meetings; instead, it must be deeply integrated into the organization's day-to-day activities, relationships, and practices. The feedback culture you build will shape how teams communicate, collaborate, and ultimately how the organization evolves over time.

The first step in creating a feedback culture is to establish clear channels for feedback. Feedback must have a defined and accessible path for everyone in the organization. In many companies, feedback is gathered in formal settings like annual reviews or retrospective meetings. While these occasions are useful, they don't provide enough of the timely, actionable input that organizations need to remain agile. Creating feedback channels that allow for quick, real-time communication makes it easier for team members to share thoughts, concerns, and suggestions. This could include using digital tools for regular surveys, instant messaging systems for quick feedback, or regular one-on-one meetings between team members and managers.

The most effective feedback channels are those that are ongoing and two-way. Feedback should flow freely in all directions—between peers, from managers to employees, and from the team to leadership. It's important that feedback isn't only solicited from the bottom up or top down, but that there is an open dialogue between all levels. A feedback culture thrives when everyone feels comfortable both giving and receiving feedback, regardless of their role or position in the hierarchy. To achieve this, leadership must model the behavior by being open to receiving feedback themselves. Leaders who seek feedback from their teams and act on it show that feedback is not a one-way street but a collaborative effort for growth.

Building trust is another fundamental element of a feedback culture. People will not share honest or constructive feedback if they do not trust that their input will be valued and acted upon. Leaders must foster a psychologically safe environment where team members feel confident sharing their thoughts without fear of retribution or negative consequences. When feedback is shared openly and respected, it builds mutual trust and respect. This trust is crucial because it encourages more transparency, deeper discussions, and ultimately better decision-making.

Feedback must also be aligned with a growth mindset. Organizations that have a feedback culture rooted in a fixed mindset, where feedback is seen as a critique or a punishment, will quickly stifle innovation and growth. Feedback should be seen as a tool for improvement, not a judgment on performance. Encouraging a growth mindset means framing feedback as an opportunity to learn and grow, rather than something to avoid or fear. Teams that approach feedback with a willingness to learn, rather than defensively protecting their actions or decisions, will not only be more agile but will also be better positioned to overcome obstacles and improve continuously.

To embed feedback into the organization's DNA, it is critical that feedback is integrated into daily processes. Instead of waiting for formal review periods, feedback should be a constant, ongoing process embedded in the everyday workflow. This can be achieved by setting clear, frequent feedback touchpoints in the form of quick check-ins, daily standups, or regular surveys. The goal is to create an environment where feedback is not seen as a rare event, but as part of the routine, ongoing improvement process.

Creating a feedback culture also means providing teams with the tools and resources they need to act on the feedback they receive. It's one thing to gather feedback, but it's another to ensure that it's implemented effectively. Teams should be empowered to take ownership of the feedback they receive, and leaders should provide the resources necessary for those changes to take place. This includes having the right tools for collaboration, project management, and tracking feedback, as well as providing time, support, and training to ensure that changes can be acted upon without delay.

Feedback should also be structured and actionable. While it's important to create opportunities for open feedback, the feedback itself needs to be focused and clear. General, vague feedback like "improve the user experience" isn't actionable. Clear, actionable feedback provides specific suggestions for improvement. For example, "The navigation menu should be more intuitive, with clearer labels and better grouping" provides actionable insights that can be implemented immediately. Teams can't act on feedback that lacks clarity or specificity, so structured feedback is essential for ensuring that ideas lead to change.

A strong feedback culture will also help teams celebrate successes. When feedback leads to improvements, it's important to recognize the efforts and contributions of individuals and teams. Celebrating successes reinforces the idea that feedback is a tool for growth and positive change, rather than something negative. Recognition helps motivate employees and builds a sense of accomplishment, while also encouraging continued engagement with feedback processes.

Leaders must commit to continuous improvement. A feedback culture requires constant nurturing and attention. Leaders must regularly check in on the state of the feedback processes, ask for input on how the feedback system could be improved, and actively listen to their teams. Feedback is not a one-time implementation—it's an ongoing process that must be continuously refined and optimized to be effective. Leaders should be committed to evolving their feedback culture just as they are committed to evolving the organization.

Creating a feedback culture is not an event but an ongoing effort to build an organization where feedback is a tool for improvement and growth. It's about establishing clear channels, building trust, creating a growth-oriented mindset, and integrating feedback into daily practices. When feedback becomes a core value, teams feel empowered, innovation thrives, and organizations can continuously adapt to meet their goals and overcome challenges. By embedding feedback into the organization's DNA, it becomes a catalyst for sustained success and long-term transformation.

THE ROLE OF FEEDBACK IN INNOVATION
How consistent feedback drives breakthroughs and accelerates growth

In any organization focused on growth and progress, innovation is key. Whether in product development, customer service, or internal processes, the ability to innovate quickly and efficiently is what keeps a company ahead of the competition. However, innovation doesn't just happen in a vacuum. It requires a continuous flow of ideas, input, and insights—this is where feedback becomes an essential part of the innovation process. Feedback acts as a mirror, reflecting the strengths and weaknesses of current initiatives, while also providing the necessary information to guide new solutions, products, and strategies.

Effective feedback loops serve as a catalyst for innovation, enabling organizations to iterate on their ideas faster, learn from mistakes sooner, and deliver better solutions more efficiently. The relationship between feedback and innovation is symbiotic. As feedback reveals areas for improvement or new opportunities, innovation fills those gaps by applying fresh ideas or adjustments. This constant exchange between feedback and innovation helps organizations move from incremental improvements to disruptive breakthroughs that reshape their industry.

One of the key benefits of incorporating feedback into the innovation process is that it allows organizations to test and validate ideas quickly. In today's world, speed is essential. The quicker an organization can test an idea and gather feedback, the quicker it can determine if that idea is worth pursuing. This is especially important in industries where market conditions and customer needs are constantly shifting. Waiting months to test a concept, only to find out it doesn't meet customer expectations, is a costly mistake. Real-time feedback loops enable teams to make adjustments on the fly, ensuring that they're always moving in the right direction.

For innovation to thrive, it's not just about gathering feedback; it's about creating a culture that values and acts on it. When feedback is integrated into the innovation process, it becomes a natural part of idea development. Teams are no longer just looking for feedback after a product launch or a project's completion; instead, they're actively seeking insights from stakeholders, customers, and even competitors throughout the development process. By building feedback into each stage of innovation—from brainstorming to prototyping to testing—teams can ensure that their solutions are always evolving and improving.

One of the challenges in fostering innovation through feedback is overcoming confirmation bias. It's human nature to look for feedback that aligns with our existing ideas and beliefs. However, for true innovation to occur, it's essential to seek out constructive criticism and alternative viewpoints. Feedback should not only affirm what is working well but also challenge assumptions and reveal blind spots. When teams are open to feedback that questions their ideas, it encourages a culture of critical thinking, where all ideas are put to the test and pushed to be better. Embracing dissenting opinions and disruptive feedback can lead to game-changing innovations that would have been impossible with a more narrow focus.

Furthermore, feedback is not just about improving existing products or processes; it's also about identifying new opportunities. Sometimes, innovation comes from unexpected sources. By seeking feedback from customers, suppliers, and even competitors, organizations can uncover needs or pain points that they hadn't considered. Customer feedback, for instance, might reveal a completely new market segment or a feature that customers didn't know they needed but would gladly adopt. Innovation often arises when organizations listen closely to the voices outside their immediate circles, gathering insights from people who experience their products in ways the creators may not have considered.

However, in order for feedback to truly drive innovation, it must be acted upon swiftly. A key aspect of an innovative feedback loop is the speed at which ideas are implemented. In traditional settings, organizations might take months or even years to make changes based on feedback. But in today's fast-paced environment, waiting to make changes means missing out on opportunities. Companies that can act on feedback quickly, whether through agile sprints, rapid prototyping, or test-and-learn methodologies, have a significant advantage over those that are slower to adapt.

Another critical factor in using feedback to fuel innovation is the alignment with organizational goals. Innovation should not be a free-for-all—ideas must be evaluated against the company's overall vision and strategic objectives. Feedback should guide teams toward solutions that align with the broader mission of the company. For example, if a company's goal is to become more sustainable, feedback that points to wasteful processes or unsustainable materials can guide teams to innovate in a way that is both efficient and aligned with the company's values. Strategic alignment ensures that the innovations resulting from feedback are not just cool ideas but are also practical, valuable, and impactful in achieving the company's long-term vision.

To truly foster a culture where feedback drives innovation, organizations must celebrate experimentation and learning. Innovation is not about getting everything right on the first try—it's about testing, failing, and iterating.

When feedback is used as a tool for learning, it shifts the mindset from perfectionism to experimentation. Teams need to feel that it's okay to fail as long as they learn and improve from those failures. This mindset encourages risk-taking, where new ideas are explored and tested without fear of making mistakes.

Feedback and innovation are not separate entities—they are deeply interconnected. Feedback serves as the fuel for innovation, providing the insights necessary to drive improvements, spark new ideas, and push boundaries. By creating systems where feedback is gathered, valued, and acted upon quickly, organizations can accelerate their innovation cycles and stay ahead of the competition. To harness the true potential of feedback, organizations must create a culture where it's actively sought, freely shared, and consistently used to improve, evolve, and create break-through solutions. In this dynamic environment, feedback becomes not just a tool for progress, but the cornerstone of an organization's ability to innovate and thrive.

TURNING FEEDBACK INTO ACTION
How to translate feedback into tangible outcomes that drive success

Collecting feedback is only half the battle—turning that feedback into actionable insights and tangible results is where the true power of feedback lies. Feedback, no matter how timely, detailed, or relevant, is only valuable if it leads to real, measurable improvements. To ensure that feedback drives success, organizations must develop a process to actively respond to it, track progress, and incorporate the learnings into their next steps.

The first critical step in turning feedback into action is to prioritize it. Feedback, especially when gathered from multiple sources, can be overwhelming. If every piece of feedback is treated as equally important, it can lead to confusion and lack of focus. To address this, feedback must be evaluated and prioritized according to the organization's goals and objectives. Not all feedback will have the same level of impact, and leaders must decide which pieces of feedback align most closely with the organization's vision and are most urgent to address. For example, feedback on a feature that negatively impacts customer satisfaction might take precedence over a minor complaint about visual design elements. The goal is to focus on feedback that can lead to the greatest improvements or offer the most significant return on investment.

Once feedback has been prioritized, the next step is to develop an action plan. Turning feedback into action requires clear planning. Simply acknowledging the feedback without a follow-up plan does little to drive change. An action plan should outline the steps needed to address the feedback, assign responsibility to specific team members, and set timelines for completion. This process ensures that feedback doesn't get lost or ignored but is actively pursued. For instance, if customer feedback indicates that a certain product feature is difficult to use, the action plan might include assigning a design team to improve the user interface, followed by a testing phase, and then releasing the update to customers. Clear steps and timelines ensure that feedback leads to tangible, timely results.

To make the action plan even more effective, it's essential to establish measurable outcomes. How will you know if the changes made based on feedback are successful? Measurable outcomes help teams track progress and assess the effectiveness of their actions. This could include customer satisfaction scores, usage rates of new features, or improved performance metrics. Establishing key performance indicators (KPIs) helps ensure that actions taken in response to feedback are actually driving progress. For example, if a product update was made in response to customer feedback, success could be measured by an increase in user engagement or a decrease in customer complaints. Regularly tracking these metrics ensures that feedback isn't just acted upon, but also evaluated for effectiveness.

Another important aspect of turning feedback into action is to close the feedback loop. Once changes have been made based on feedback, it's crucial to follow up with the individuals or groups who provided that feedback to let them know what actions have been taken. Closing the feedback loop not only shows that feedback is valued, but it also builds trust. When customers, employees, or other stakeholders see that their input leads to real change, they are more likely to provide valuable feedback in the future. This also encourages continued engagement with feedback mechanisms, ensuring that the process of improvement is ongoing.

Continuous improvement is the goal of feedback-driven action. The process of turning feedback into action should not be a one-time event, but an ongoing cycle. As changes are made, new feedback will arise, and the cycle starts again. This creates a culture of continuous improvement, where every iteration is an opportunity to refine and optimize processes, products, and services. By embedding feedback loops into the organization's regular workflow, feedback becomes an inherent part of how the organization evolves and improves over time.

To facilitate continuous improvement, organizations should also celebrate successes. When feedback leads to positive changes, it's important to recognize and celebrate those successes. This not only boosts morale but reinforces the value of feedback. When teams and individuals see the positive impact of their work, they are motivated to continue seeking and responding to feedback. Recognition can take many forms, from acknowledging team achievements in meetings to celebrating milestones in the product development process. Celebrating successes helps maintain momentum and encourages a feedback culture where everyone is motivated to contribute to improvements.

Feedback should be integrated into decision-making processes. To truly turn feedback into action, it must become a key input in the decision-making process, not just something that is collected and filed away. This means making feedback a core part of strategic planning, product development, and organizational development. For example, product managers should actively solicit feedback from customers during the design phase, not just at the end of a project. Leaders should include feedback when making high-level decisions about the future direction of the organization. By embedding feedback into the decision-making process, it becomes part of the DNA of the organization, ensuring that it drives change at all levels. Turning feedback into action requires prioritization, action planning, measurable outcomes, feedback loops, continuous improvement, celebration of success, and integration into decision-making processes. Feedback is not just an end-of-project task but an ongoing process that informs the direction of the organization and drives continuous growth. When feedback is acted upon quickly, efficiently, and strategically, it becomes a powerful tool for change, helping organizations adapt, innovate, and thrive in an ever-evolving landscape.

PART IV
Sustaining the Momentum

FROM LAUNCH TO LEGACY: KEEPING CHANGE ALIVE

As any leader or transformation agent knows, the most challenging part of any journey is ensuring that the momentum created in the early stages of a project or transformation continues long after the initial excitement fades. It's easy to get caught up in the thrill of new ideas, innovative projects, and the beginning stages of change. But sustaining that energy over time, when challenges inevitably arise and the novelty wears off, is where the true work begins.

The work of transformation doesn't end once new systems, processes, or products are launched—it's just the beginning. The challenge is ensuring that the momentum doesn't dissipate but instead becomes an enduring force that drives long-term success and growth. To make change stick, it must be continuously reinforced, re-evaluated, and nurtured over time.

In this part of the book, we'll explore how to keep that

momentum alive through a combination of consistent habits, resilience in the face of uncertainty, and leadership strategies that scale your impact. Sustaining momentum isn't about doing the same things over and over; it's about building the systems and structures that allow change to thrive over time.

The biggest hurdle to sustaining momentum is the natural tendency for organizations to revert back to the status quo when challenges arise. Old habits die hard, and without proper guidance, the initial gains made through transformation can be lost. But the true power of transformation lies in its ability to evolve, adapt, and build on the foundations you've already set. Sustaining momentum is a continuous process of small, strategic steps that reinforce and amplify the changes you've already initiated.

This section will also focus on how to lead through uncertainty, a crucial skill in today's ever-changing environment. Transformation initiatives are rarely linear. They often encounter bumps, setbacks, and even resistance. Leaders who are able to navigate these challenges and keep the team focused on the long-term goals are crucial to ensuring that transformation efforts don't stall.

Lastly, we'll discuss how to scale your leadership as the transformation expands. As the change grows, the leader's role shifts from being directly involved in day-to-day tasks to guiding, mentoring, and ensuring that the new systems and behaviors are scaled and embedded at every level of the organization.

In summary, sustaining momentum is the art of maintaining energy, focus, and drive long after the initial phase of transformation has passed. It's about building habits that endure, embracing uncertainty, and growing your leadership to ensure that change is not only sustained but continues to evolve and grow over time. This part of the book is about preparing your organization to thrive in the long term, not just survive the transformation.

Change as a Habit

CREATING RITUALS AND RHYTHMS FOR LASTING
TRANSFORMATION

THE HABIT OF CHANGE
How small, consistent actions build long-term transformation

One of the biggest challenges organizations face when undergoing transformation is making change stick. Often, a company might experience initial success during the early stages of transformation, but without the right support, those changes can fade away over time. This is where the power of habit comes into play. For lasting transformation to occur, change needs to become a regular, automatic part of an organization's culture and practices. It needs to become a habit—something employees do consistently without even thinking about it.

The key to creating a habit of change is to focus on small, consistent actions. Often, leaders and organizations are tempted to focus on grand, sweeping changes that promise to deliver immediate results. However, lasting change rarely happens overnight. Instead, it happens incrementally, through a series of small actions that, over time, compound and create a significant impact. The key is to focus on making those small actions a natural part of the day-to-day operations.

This concept can be applied to any aspect of organizational change—whether it's shifting to a new way of working, implementing new technologies, or changing the company culture. The goal is not to rely on periodic changes or isolated initiatives, but to embed new behaviors into the regular rhythm of the organization. Just like brushing your teeth every morning or going for a run, organizational habits should become something employees do without thinking twice. For example, if collaboration is a key part of your transformation strategy, the habit should be to meet regularly, share knowledge across departments, and continuously evaluate team dynamics to improve collaboration.

One of the most important elements of creating the habit of change is consistency. In the beginning stages of a transformation, enthusiasm may be high, and everyone is eager to implement new ideas. But as time goes on and challenges arise, it's easy for teams to revert to old habits or forget the new processes altogether. This is why consistency is crucial. Leaders must make sure that the behaviors they want to establish as habits are reinforced regularly. Whether it's through weekly check-ins, daily stand-ups, or monthly performance reviews, regular reinforcement helps keep the change top of mind and ensures that it becomes ingrained in the organization's daily rhythm.

Another key component of turning change into a habit is making the change part of the organization's systems and processes. For instance, if an organization is shifting to an agile methodology, the practices and tools associated with agile should not just be optional or occasional. They should be embedded in every project, with clear structures in place to ensure that agile practices are followed throughout. Similarly, if you want to build a culture of continuous feedback, feedback loops should be woven into every team meeting, every project sprint, and even day-to-day interactions. By embedding these new behaviors into existing workflows, the changes become less like a one-time intervention and more like an automatic, ongoing process.

Creating a habit of change also requires making the new behaviors simple and easy to adopt. Complexity is one of the biggest barriers to behavior change. If the new way of working is too complicated or difficult to implement, employees will quickly fall back on old habits. The simpler and more intuitive the change, the easier it is to integrate into the organization's everyday activities. For example, when adopting new software tools or technologies, it's important to prioritize user-friendliness and clear onboarding processes. The simpler the process, the more likely employees are to adopt the change as part of their daily routine.

Reinforcement is another critical factor in making change a habit. It's not enough to simply implement new behaviors and expect them to stick on their own. You must continuously reinforce those behaviors to ensure they continue over time. One way to do this is by celebrating small wins. Acknowledging progress—whether it's completing a successful sprint or making progress toward a key milestone—reinforces the idea that the change is having a positive impact and motivates employees to continue the new behavior. Celebrating success also helps keep employees engaged and committed to the transformation, making the process more enjoyable and less of a burden.

Feedback is another powerful tool in reinforcing new habits. Leaders should seek regular feedback on how well the changes are being implemented, what's working, and where improvements are needed. Feedback from employees helps leaders gauge how effectively the changes are being integrated into daily operations and whether any adjustments are necessary. Additionally, recognizing feedback when it leads to positive change ensures that employees feel heard and valued, which can further strengthen their commitment to the new behaviors.

CREATING RITUALS AND RHYTHMS
How to establish regular practices that reinforce change and make it sustainable

Building lasting change requires more than just shifting behaviors temporarily. It's about creating a ritualistic rhythm that reinforces the change over time and becomes part of the organizational fabric. Rituals and rhythms help transform what may initially seem like an arduous shift into something that feels natural, routine, and even automatic. These rituals act as the backbone of change, providing a structured approach that guides the organization in the right direction without requiring constant effort or decision-making.

A key part of creating these rituals is identifying the behaviors that need to become habitual. Every organization is unique, so the rituals that work for one may not work for another. However, certain core practices can be universal. For instance, one of the first rituals that an organization should introduce is the regular reflection and evaluation of progress. This could take the form of weekly check-ins, monthly reviews, or quarterly planning sessions. These rituals create a structured opportunity to assess how the transformation is progressing and ensure that the new behaviors are becoming deeply ingrained. Regular reflection not only helps identify obstacles but also provides a platform for sharing successes and learning from mistakes.

In the same vein, creating rituals around communication is critical. Clear and consistent communication must be a part of the organization's transformation rituals. Leaders should prioritize open dialogue, where team members can voice concerns, provide feedback, and share insights. Communication rituals can take many forms: from team meetings and daily stand-ups to virtual communication tools that allow real-time updates and transparency. Regular communication helps keep everyone on the same page, ensuring that the change remains visible, top of mind, and aligned with organizational goals.

Another important aspect of rituals is the celebration of small wins. These celebrations should be embedded into the culture as a ritual in and of themselves. Every milestone achieved, whether big or small, deserves recognition. These celebrations act as positive reinforcement for new behaviors and provide motivation to continue the effort. Whether it's completing a successful sprint, hitting a target, or solving a difficult problem, public acknowledgment of these wins reinforces the idea that progress is being made. Celebrating successes also helps build momentum and keeps the team excited about the transformation.

Rituals related to learning and improvement should also be a core part of the organization's daily rhythm. In an ever-changing world, the only constant is change itself, and the ability to adapt and learn is a vital part of sustaining that change. Organizations must create a rhythm around continuous learning, where employees are encouraged to reflect, experiment, and grow. Whether this involves structured training sessions, peer-to-peer learning, or self-paced development opportunities, making learning a regular part of the organizational ritual helps ensure that employees remain flexible, adaptable, and ready to take on new challenges.

Beyond formal rituals, informal rhythms also play a role in reinforcing change. These can be spontaneous moments where employees gather to share ideas, discuss challenges, or simply connect with one another. Informal rituals, such as collaborative brainstorming sessions or even casual coffee breaks where team members can chat and share insights, help foster the human side of change. These informal connections can inspire new ideas and spark creative solutions to challenges that might not emerge in more structured settings. They also create a culture of collaboration and community, which is critical when trying to instill change in an organization.

The regularity of these rituals is important. Without consistency, even the best rituals can become ineffective. Change must be woven into the rhythm of everyday life within the organization. This means making rituals frequent enough that they become second nature. If feedback loops are only conducted quarterly, for instance, they may lose their impact, and the organization may revert to old habits. Instead, feedback should be sought frequently— on a weekly or even daily basis—to keep the momentum of change alive. Similarly, learning and celebration should be consistent, so they feel like integral parts of the team's routine, not occasional events.

Another critical part of rituals and rhythms is ensuring that they are aligned with the organization's vision and values. Rituals are not just about adopting new behaviors —they are about creating behaviors that support the organization's strategic goals and cultural values. If a company values innovation, for example, the rituals might include brainstorming sessions or "hackathons" that encourage employees to think outside the box and push creative boundaries. If customer-centricity is a priority, rituals might revolve around regularly collecting and acting on customer feedback. By aligning rituals with the organization's core values, you ensure that change isn't just cosmetic but is deeply embedded in the way the organization functions.

It's also important to ensure that leaders model these rituals. Change can't be imposed from the top down—it must be lived from the top down. When leaders consistently participate in the rituals they've established, they set the tone for the rest of the organization. Leaders must actively engage in communication rituals, feedback loops, celebrations, and learning opportunities, demonstrating the behaviors they want to see in others. Their commitment to these rituals reinforces the message that change is not just a temporary initiative but a long-term way of working.

Rituals must evolve. As the organization transforms and grows, the rituals themselves should be refined to remain relevant. A ritual that served the organization well in its early stages of change may need to be adjusted as the organization matures and the transformation deepens. Regularly evaluating and adjusting the rituals ensures that they stay aligned with the organization's evolving needs and goals.

MAINTAINING MOMENTUM OVER TIME
How to keep the energy alive and prevent transformation fatigue

One of the greatest challenges organizations face after initiating a transformation is maintaining momentum. It's easy to start strong, fueled by excitement and the promise of new opportunities, but over time, the initial enthusiasm can dwindle. As teams encounter setbacks, frustration can build, and the transformation that was once seen as an exciting adventure may begin to feel like a heavy burden. This is why sustaining momentum is essential for long-term success. Without ongoing energy and focus, even the best-laid plans can falter.

The first step to maintaining momentum is to reaffirm the purpose behind the transformation. In the early stages, the reasons for the change are usually clear: a new strategy, technology, or structure that will help the organization grow and adapt to the future. However, as the process continues, it can become easy to lose sight of why the change was needed in the first place. Regularly reminding the team of the vision and the desired outcomes keeps everyone aligned and focused on the bigger picture. Whether through internal communications, leadership speeches, or team meetings, leaders should consistently bring the focus back to the mission, ensuring that everyone understands how their efforts contribute to the overall goals.

To keep energy high, celebrating progress is critical. While transformational change is often long-term, small wins should be recognized and celebrated. These can be milestones reached in the project, positive feedback from customers, or any notable improvement resulting from the transformation. Celebrating these successes, no matter how small, keeps the team motivated and reinforces the idea that progress is happening, even if it's incremental. These celebrations act as markers along the transformation journey, creating a sense of achievement and a reminder that the change is working.

However, while celebrating wins is important, leaders must also acknowledge the difficulties and challenges that come with transformation. Transformation is rarely a smooth, uninterrupted process. There will be setbacks, roadblocks, and moments of frustration. By acknowledging the tough moments and showing empathy toward the challenges employees face, leaders can build trust and foster a sense of shared commitment. Transparency in addressing challenges helps prevent burnout by showing the team that obstacles are part of the process, and that they can be overcome.

Equally important is ensuring that the organization has the resources and support to sustain the transformation. Often, organizations will allocate resources at the start of the transformation and then let them dwindle as the process continues. To avoid this, organizations must commit to sustaining investment in key areas such as technology, training, and talent development. Providing the necessary tools and support ensures that employees are equipped to handle the changes and continue moving forward with confidence.

Empowering employees is another key strategy in maintaining momentum. When employees are given ownership of the transformation process, they are more likely to stay engaged and invested in its success. Delegating responsibilities and involving employees in decision-making creates a sense of ownership and accountability. This is particularly important in an agile environment, where teams must constantly adapt to new information.

When employees feel empowered to make decisions and contribute to the transformation, they are more likely to stay motivated and enthusiastic, even during difficult phases of the process.

Maintaining momentum also requires leaders to regularly check in on progress. While it's important to acknowledge the milestones, it's equally important to track progress consistently. Leaders should monitor whether the goals set at the beginning of the transformation are being met and whether the changes are leading to the desired outcomes. Adjustments should be made as necessary, especially if feedback from employees or customers indicates that the transformation is not progressing as expected. Regular check-ins allow leaders to catch issues early and address them before they become larger problems.

Another strategy to sustain momentum is revisiting the transformation's value proposition. At the beginning of a transformation, the benefits are often clear and exciting—improving customer experience, increasing efficiency, or positioning the company for growth. But as the process goes on, these benefits can become abstract or lost in the day-to-day grind. Leaders should periodically revisit these benefits with the team, ensuring everyone understands why the transformation matters and how it will benefit them personally and professionally. By continually reinforcing the personal and professional benefits of the change, employees are more likely to remain committed and engaged.

MAKING CHANGE LAST
How to ensure that the changes made during transformation are sustainable in the long run

Transformations are dynamic, and while they may begin with a surge of energy, that initial excitement can often diminish over time. Sustaining change requires a shift in mindset—moving from short-term efforts to long-term, consistent actions that become embedded in the organization's culture. Without careful planning and ongoing commitment, the changes made during a transformation can fade, and the organization risks falling back into old, inefficient habits. To prevent this, organizations need to build the structural and cultural support necessary to ensure the changes endure.

One of the most important strategies for making change last is embedding the transformation into the daily routine. Transformation efforts often fail when they are seen as one-off projects or external initiatives, separate from the core activities of the organization. To make change sustainable, it must be integrated into the routine operations of the company. This means that the new processes, systems, or behaviors must be reflected in the daily practices of employees, leaders, and teams. For example, if part of the transformation is the adoption of a new technology, it should become a core part of the daily workflow, not just something employees use occasionally. The goal is for employees to feel that the transformation is not an added burden but a natural progression that improves their work.

A critical element of embedding transformation into daily routines is to focus on habits and rituals. Much like personal habits, the habits formed in an organization are hard to break. If a company successfully creates habits around new ways of working, they will continue even in times of stress or uncertainty. Whether it's a daily stand-up meeting, a weekly review session, or regular feedback loops, these rituals help to reinforce the desired changes and make them part of the organizational rhythm. Over time, these rituals become automatic, requiring little effort to maintain, and they keep the focus on the goals of the transformation.

While rituals are crucial, accountability is another essential component in sustaining change. Change cannot be left to chance. There must be clear expectations and ownership over specific outcomes. This means setting measurable targets and holding individuals and teams accountable for achieving them. Accountability encourages consistent follow-through and ensures that the transformation is not sidelined as other priorities emerge. It is critical that accountability goes hand in hand with the organization's overall vision for change. When leaders hold themselves and their teams accountable, it reinforces that the transformation is an ongoing commitment and not just a passing trend.

A major obstacle to sustained change is resistance, which can arise at various stages of transformation. When the excitement of new changes begins to fade, individuals or groups within the organization may become resistant to the ongoing transformation. Some might miss old processes, while others may simply feel overwhelmed by the pace of change. The key to overcoming resistance is consistent communication. Leaders must continue to articulate the reasons for change, remind employees of the value it brings, and acknowledge the challenges that accompany transformation. By maintaining an open dialogue and listening to concerns, leaders can mitigate resistance and encourage employees to stay engaged in the change process.

Regularly acknowledging and celebrating progress is another important strategy for making change last. People are more likely to remain motivated when they see that their efforts are making a tangible difference. Leaders should ensure that achievements—both big and small—are recognized and celebrated. This can range from a formal celebration of a successful product launch to informal recognition during team meetings. Acknowledging progress reinforces the idea that change is working, which helps maintain momentum and boosts morale. Celebrations also provide an opportunity to reflect on what has been achieved, creating a positive feedback loop that fuels further progress.

However, recognizing success should never mean resting on laurels. For change to be sustainable, organizations must embrace a mindset of continuous improvement. Transformation is not a destination—it's a journey. Even after the initial goals are achieved, there will always be room for improvement. Teams should be encouraged to continue innovating, adapting, and optimizing processes. By fostering a culture where continuous learning is valued, organizations can stay ahead of the curve and avoid complacency. This involves creating systems for feedback, evaluation, and iteration so that the organization never stops refining its practices and aligning with emerging trends.

Creating a feedback-rich environment also involves making feedback loops integral to the change process. Feedback should not just be gathered at set points or at the end of a transformation project—it should be a continuous process that informs ongoing change. Regular feedback provides insights into areas of strength as well as areas for improvement. It's vital that organizations use feedback to adapt and make real-time adjustments, ensuring that the transformation continues to align with the organization's evolving needs and goals. Regular feedback mechanisms allow teams to monitor their progress and pivot as needed, reinforcing that change is a living, breathing process.

Equally important in sustaining change is ensuring that the leadership remains committed to the transformation, no matter how much time has passed. Leadership involvement should not wane once the initial excitement of the transformation has faded. Leaders must continuously support and champion the change, ensuring that it remains a strategic priority for the organization. Leadership visibility is crucial in maintaining the focus on transformation. Whether it's through regular communications, town hall meetings, or walking the floor to connect with employees, leaders must remain visible and actively engaged in the transformation process.

Leading Through Uncertainty

HOW TO HANDLE DOUBT, RESISTANCE, AND AMBIGUITY

EMBRACING AMBIGUITY
Why uncertainty is an opportunity, not a threat

One of the hallmarks of leading through times of transformation is the uncertainty that inevitably arises. Whether it's changes in market conditions, shifting customer expectations, or the complexity of internal changes, leaders must navigate through periods of ambiguity and confusion. The common instinct in times of uncertainty is to seek immediate clarity, to remove all ambiguity. However, uncertainty is not something to fear—it is something to embrace. In fact, uncertainty can be one of the greatest sources of opportunity for growth and innovation.

Uncertainty often triggers fear and resistance—both of which can block progress. When people are faced with unknowns, they tend to react by retreating to the safety of what they know, which may prevent them from fully engaging with the change process. However, uncertainty can also be a breeding ground for creative solutions, problem-solving, and innovation. It's in these periods of ambiguity that teams can reimagine possibilities, challenge established norms, and explore new ways of working. Instead of reacting to uncertainty with fear or resistance, great leaders embrace it as an opportunity to encourage exploration, foster creativity, and drive positive change.

A leader's role during times of uncertainty is to provide a sense of direction and purpose, even when the exact details are not yet clear. While it's important to acknowledge that the future is unpredictable, leaders can still provide clarity in terms of vision and values. By focusing on the bigger picture—the long-term goals of the organization and the values that will guide decisions—leaders can offer a sense of security to their teams. Clarity of purpose helps teams feel grounded and oriented, even when specific outcomes are uncertain.

Another way leaders can effectively navigate ambiguity is by encouraging resilience within their teams. Resilience is the ability to adapt and bounce back when faced with setbacks, obstacles, or changes. When uncertainty arises, resilient teams do not become immobilized by doubt or fear; instead, they remain flexible, resourceful, and willing to pivot when necessary. By fostering a resilient mindset, leaders can ensure that their teams stay motivated and engaged, even when the path forward is unclear. Resilience also empowers individuals to approach uncertainty with confidence, knowing they can handle whatever challenges arise.

It's also important for leaders to stay calm and be transparent in moments of uncertainty. The natural human response to ambiguity is anxiety, and employees will look to their leaders for cues on how to react. If leaders appear to be panicking or uncertain themselves, it can amplify fears throughout the organization. Conversely, when leaders remain calm, composed, and honest about the challenges, it helps to instill confidence in the team. Transparency—about what is known, what is uncertain, and the steps being taken to navigate challenges—helps to reduce anxiety and ensures that teams feel empowered to work through the ambiguity together.

NAVIGATING RESISTANCE
How to address and overcome resistance to change in the organization

Resistance is one of the most natural responses to change, and it can manifest in many forms—whether it's open pushback, passive disengagement, or even silent sabotage. In a transformation process, especially when the changes are significant or affect established routines, it's almost inevitable that some form of resistance will surface. Understanding that resistance is normal and part of the change process is crucial for leaders. However, how leaders address and manage that resistance can make or break the transformation.

One of the first steps in addressing resistance is to acknowledge it openly. Often, resistance is dismissed or ignored, with the hope that it will eventually dissipate. However, ignoring resistance only leads to it growing in intensity, potentially derailing the entire transformation effort. Leaders must embrace resistance as an opportunity for dialogue, rather than as a barrier to progress. Openly acknowledging that change is difficult and that resistance is a natural part of the process can help to validate concerns and demonstrate empathy. When people feel heard and understood, they are more likely to open up, share their concerns, and engage in a productive discussion.

Another effective approach to managing resistance is to identify the root causes. Resistance doesn't always stem from a lack of understanding or commitment to the change itself. In many cases, resistance arises from deeper concerns, such as fear of job loss, a perceived threat to power or autonomy, or uncertainty about the outcomes of the change. By asking the right questions and listening attentively to the concerns of employees, leaders can uncover the true sources of resistance. This allows them to address those concerns directly, rather than merely treating the symptoms. For example, if employees are resisting a new technology, it may not be because they oppose the tool itself, but because they fear they don't have the skills to use it effectively. In this case, offering training and providing adequate support can significantly reduce resistance.

Clear communication is essential in overcoming resistance. People often resist change when they don't fully understand why it is happening, how it will impact them, or what the ultimate goals are. Leaders must be transparent about the reasons for the change, the expected benefits, and the plan for implementation. When employees understand the bigger picture—why the change is necessary and how it aligns with organizational goals— they are more likely to accept it. Additionally, leaders should actively engage in two-way communication, allowing team members to voice their concerns and ask questions. This helps to build trust and reduces fear and anxiety around the unknown. Frequent updates about progress and challenges also keep everyone informed and reduce uncertainty.

Resistance can also be mitigated by involving employees in the change process. People are more likely to support a change when they feel like they have a say in it. Leaders should strive to make employees part of the solution, rather than just passive recipients of the change. This can be done by involving employees in decision-making, soliciting their ideas, and empowering them to take ownership of certain aspects of the transformation. When employees feel empowered and involved, their resistance decreases, and they become active contributors to the change process. This level of engagement fosters owner-ship, which is a powerful antidote to resistance.

Leaders must also provide support systems throughout the transformation. Change can feel overwhelming, and without proper support, employees may feel isolated or ill-equipped to navigate the new landscape. Offering support in the form of training, mentoring, or even peer networks can alleviate some of the stress that comes with change. Leaders should ensure that employees have the resources they need to succeed, whether it's through additional skills development, access to new tools, or guidance from mentors. When employees feel that they are being supported through the process, their fear of the unknown diminishes, and their resistance weakens.

Recognizing and addressing emotional resistance is another critical step. People often resist change not because of the logical aspects of the transformation, but because of emotional factors such as fear, insecurity, or frustration. Change can trigger deep emotions, especially when it involves significant shifts in roles, responsibilities, or ways of working. Leaders must acknowledge these emotional responses and create a safe space for employees to express their feelings. By allowing employees to share their concerns and frustrations, leaders can help them process these emotions and move forward. This can be done through one-on-one conversations, group discussions, or even informal check-ins to assess the emotional well-being of the team.

Leading by example is also crucial in overcoming resis-tance. Employees are more likely to embrace change when they see their leaders fully committed to it. If leaders appear hesitant, reluctant, or disengaged, it sends the message that the change is not important or worth embracing. Leaders must model the behaviors they want to see in others, showing commitment, positivity, and resilience in the face of challenges. When employees see their leaders taking risks, engaging with the change, and demonstrating a willingness to learn and adapt, they are more likely to follow suit.

NAVIGATING THROUGH DOUBT
How to maintain confidence and clarity during times of uncertainty

Doubt is an inevitable part of any transformation process, and it's especially prevalent when organizations face significant change. It can creep in at various stages—whether it's uncertainty about the outcomes, lack of confidence in the new direction, or simply the anxiety that comes with the unknown. For leaders, handling doubt is a critical skill, because if left unaddressed, it can quickly become contagious and spread throughout the organization. It's important to recognize that while doubt is a natural response, it doesn't have to derail progress. Instead, it can serve as an opportunity for reflection, clarification, and reaffirmation.

When doubt arises, the first step is to acknowledge it. Many leaders may be tempted to ignore or downplay doubt, especially if they feel they need to project unwavering confidence. However, ignoring doubt doesn't make it disappear—it simply allows it to fester and grow. Acknowledging doubt helps create an environment where transparency and open dialogue are prioritized. Leaders should address the elephant in the room, acknowledging that the transformation process is challenging and uncertain. By doing so, they validate the concerns of their teams, which can lead to a more constructive conversation and help alleviate anxiety.

After acknowledging doubt, the next step is to provide clarity and direction. One of the main reasons doubt flourishes during times of transformation is due to a lack of clarity. When employees are unsure of the transformation's goals, their role in the process, or how the changes will affect them, doubt can quickly set in. Leaders must work to provide clear, consistent communication that helps remove ambiguity. This means not only explaining the "what" and "how" of the change but also the "why"—why the change is necessary, how it aligns with the organization's vision, and the impact it will have on employees and customers. When leaders reaffirm the purpose of the transformation and connect it to the company's core values, it helps to dispel doubt and builds confidence in the direction.

Another essential strategy for navigating doubt is to build resilience within teams. When uncertainty strikes, resilient teams are better equipped to handle setbacks and continue making progress. Leaders should focus on fostering resilience by encouraging a mindset of adaptability and problem-solving. This can be achieved by creating an environment where failure is viewed as an opportunity to learn rather than a setback. By framing doubt and uncertainty as challenges to be overcome rather than insurmountable obstacles, leaders help teams maintain focus and stay committed to the transformation journey.

Moreover, leaders must be authentic and transparent in how they manage doubt. Confidence is crucial, but it must be grounded in honesty and integrity. When leaders are transparent about the challenges the organization is facing, including their own uncertainties, they model vulnerability and create space for others to share their concerns. This builds trust and reinforces the idea that doubt is a natural part of growth. For example, if there are delays in the transformation timeline or unexpected obstacles, leaders should be upfront about the situation, while also outlining the steps being taken to address the issues. Being authentic about doubt doesn't mean giving up on the vision—it means showing resilience in the face of adversity.

Another important aspect of handling doubt is to focus on incremental progress rather than expecting instant results. Transformations are rarely linear, and they don't always follow a clear, predictable path. Leaders must help teams understand that progress is often achieved through small, cumulative steps, and that even setbacks or periods of stagnation are part of the process. By setting short-term goals and celebrating small wins, leaders can maintain momentum and counteract feelings of doubt. These milestones remind the team that progress is being made, even if it's not immediately obvious. Regularly highlighting achievements—whether it's a successful product launch, positive customer feedback, or a milestone in the change process—reassures teams that they are moving in the right direction, even when the road ahead may still seem uncertain.

Additionally, leaders can help reduce doubt by providing support and reassurance to their teams. Transformation is stressful, and it can take a toll on employees' mental and emotional well-being. Leaders must ensure that employees feel supported through the process by offering the necessary resources, training, and encouragement. Creating a safe space for employees to voice their concerns or ask questions without judgment fosters a culture of trust and ensures that doubt can be addressed openly. Leaders should also encourage peer support, as team members can often provide reassurance and perspective that leaders might not be able to offer. Whether through informal check-ins, mentorship, or collaboration, providing support helps reduce feelings of doubt and encourages a sense of unity and collective purpose.

It's important for leaders to recognize that doubt is not necessarily a negative force. While it can certainly be disruptive, doubt also serves as a natural reaction to the unknown. Leaders who understand the role doubt plays in the change process are better positioned to manage it effectively and use it to their advantage. Doubt can act as a check on assumptions, encouraging reflection and ensuring that the organization is truly addressing the most pressing issues. Healthy skepticism can lead to more thoughtful decision-making, better solutions, and stronger buy-in from employees, as they feel they are part of a more inclusive and honest process.

RESISTING BACKSLIDE
How to prevent the organization from reverting to old habits

Change is difficult. Even when the initial stages of transformation are met with enthusiasm and positive momentum, the real challenge often comes after the transformation has been implemented. This is when many organizations experience a backslide, reverting to old ways of doing things. It's easy to assume that once a new way of working is established, it's here to stay. However, unless there is a structured approach to ensuring the new behaviors and practices are continually reinforced, the organization risks falling back into familiar routines and habits that may no longer serve its long-term goals.

To resist backslide, organizations must build in guardrails to keep the new behaviors alive and ensure that they are not just temporary changes. A crucial first step in preventing backslide is to reaffirm the vision and the purpose of the transformation regularly. Repeatedly emphasizing the "why" behind the change reminds employees of the benefits of the new ways of working and reinforces the long-term goals that they are striving toward. Constant reminders of the vision also help keep employees focused and prevent them from losing sight of the bigger picture. It's easy to get caught up in daily challenges or revert to old habits when the larger goal is not consistently reinforced.

Leaders should also monitor behaviors closely to ensure the changes are taking hold. Tracking progress in terms of both quantitative metrics and qualitative feedback gives a clear picture of how well the transformation is sticking. Regular check-ins, performance evaluations, and feedback loops help leaders identify whether employees are adopting the new behaviors. This ongoing monitoring should not be used as a tool for micromanagement but rather as an opportunity for celebrating progress and identifying areas for improvement. If the new behaviors are not being implemented as intended, leaders can act quickly to provide guidance, training, or resources to course-correct.

One of the most effective ways to prevent backslide is to empower employees to hold each other accountable. When people are part of the change process and actively involved in making the transformation a success, they are more likely to hold one another to the standards and behaviors set out by the organization. Accountability should not rest solely on leadership; employees should be encouraged to check in with each other and provide constructive feedback. Creating a culture of peer accountability allows employees to work together to reinforce the changes, preventing old habits from creeping back in. This also helps build a sense of ownership and collective responsibility for the success of the transformation.

Another strategy to prevent backslide is to celebrate the integration of new behaviors into the organizational culture. When new practices become part of the culture, they are less likely to be abandoned. This can be achieved by weaving the new behaviors into performance reviews, recognition programs, and company rituals. For instance, if one of the goals of the transformation is improved collaboration, celebrating cross-departmental projects or collaborative efforts during company-wide meetings sends a powerful message that these behaviors are valued and should be continued. Recognizing and rewarding those who exemplify the desired behaviors makes it clear that these actions are integral to the success of the organization.

Additionally, it's important to address complacency.

Over time, the excitement around a transformation tends to fade, and some employees may begin to feel that the change is complete or that the hard work is done. This complacency can lead to a slow reversion to old habits. Leaders need to make sure that the change process is ongoing, with opportunities for continuous learning and improvement. Providing regular opportunities for employees to refresh their knowledge, skills, and commitment to the transformation keeps the momentum going. This could involve refresher courses, coaching sessions, or revisiting the goals of the transformation during team meetings. By ensuring that employees stay engaged with the transformation process, organizations can combat complacency and keep old habits from resurfacing.

Another important step is to reinforce the behavior with systems and tools. The new practices and behaviors that the organization wants to instill should be supported by the systems and tools employees use every day. For example, if the transformation includes a shift to more collaborative project management or cross-functional teamwork, then the tools used (e.g., project management software, communication platforms) should support and facilitate these behaviors. Systems and processes that reinforce the new way of working will help make those behaviors habitual. This can also include aligning incentives and performance metrics with the behaviors the organization wants to promote. When systems are aligned with desired changes, it's much easier for employees to follow through.

To effectively prevent backslide, constant reinforcement is necessary. Just as the organization worked hard to implement the transformation in the first place, maintaining it requires ongoing effort. Leaders should make the new behaviors a part of daily conversations, team meetings, and organizational rituals. For example, leaders can introduce regular check-ins to ensure that the changes are still being implemented, provide support and guidance as needed, and continually celebrate progress toward the desired outcomes. Ensuring that the new behaviors are constantly reinforced through repetition helps them become ingrained in the organization's culture.

BUILDING A CHANGE-CENTRIC
ORGANIZATION
How to cultivate an environment where change is embraced as the norm

A fundamental challenge of any transformation is creating a work environment that is flexible, agile, and prepared for continuous change. Without the right foundation, any transformation—no matter how well executed—can be a short-term effort. The key to ensuring lasting and successful transformation is to build an organization that embraces change as a norm rather than a temporary state. This requires a deliberate effort to create an organizational culture where change is not feared but is actively welcomed as an opportunity for growth, innovation, and improvement.

The first step in building a change-centric organization is to shift the organizational mindset. In many traditional organizations, change is viewed as an anomaly or an event that must be managed. However, in a change-centric organization, change becomes an integral part of the organizational DNA. Leadership must foster a growth mindset across all levels of the organization, where employees see challenges and changes as opportunities to learn and evolve rather than as threats. The goal is to normalize change by making it part of the everyday workflow, and to help everyone see change as a tool for continuous improvement rather than something that disrupts stability.

In a change-centric organization, leaders play a critical role in modeling and reinforcing the behaviors that align with a change-oriented culture. Leadership must lead by example, demonstrating flexibility, adaptability, and a willingness to take risks. Leaders should embrace a mindset that allows them to reframe failure as a learning experience, not as a setback. When leaders model this behavior, it sets the tone for the entire organization. Employees are more likely to adopt the same approach if they see that their leaders are resilient in the face of adversity and focused on long-term growth. Encouraging experimentation, allowing teams to try new approaches, and celebrating learning from failure are key aspects of leadership in a change-centric environment.

One of the key components of building a change-centric culture is empowering employees at all levels. A culture of change is not just about top-down direction; it's about enabling every individual in the organization to take ownership of change and contribute to the process. Empowering employees means giving them the authority and responsibility to make decisions, to experiment with new ideas, and to challenge the status quo. This requires trust and transparency from leadership, as well as the willingness to delegate authority and support innovation at all levels of the organization. When employees feel empowered to make decisions and have the autonomy to implement their own ideas, they become active participants in the transformation process rather than passive recipients of change.

Additionally, open communication is essential for building a change-centric organization. Communication helps to eliminate ambiguity and uncertainty, which are common barriers to embracing change. Regular communication from leadership—whether through town hall meetings, internal newsletters, or team check-ins—helps ensure that everyone in the organization is aligned and informed about the change process. Communication should be two-way, allowing employees to share their ideas, feedback, and concerns. Leaders should actively listen to their teams and incorporate their input into the change process. When feedback is encouraged and valued, employees feel more involved in the transformation and are more likely to support it. Communication is not just about what is said, but about creating a dialogue where all voices are heard and respected.

As organizations grow and evolve, it's also important to celebrate change and its impact. By celebrating milestones and acknowledging progress, organizations reinforce the importance of change and the benefits it brings. Celebrations could take many forms, such as team celebrations after a successful project, company-wide recognition of innovation, or informal recognition of employees who have made significant contributions to the change process. Recognizing and celebrating success helps to build momentum and encourages employees to stay engaged and motivated. When people see the tangible impact of change, it strengthens their commitment to continuing to improve.

Training and development are also essential in cultivating a change-centric organization. As organizations evolve, so too must the skills and knowledge of their workforce. Providing ongoing training and development opportunities ensures that employees are well-equipped to handle the changes being introduced. This can include anything from technical training on new tools and systems, to leadership development programs that teach employees how to lead and manage change themselves. Equipping employees with the right skills to navigate change empowers them to embrace it with confidence, rather than fear. Training and development also signal to employees that the organization is investing in their growth, which strengthens loyalty and commitment to the transformation.

It's also important to align the organization's reward and recognition systems with the goals of change. Traditional reward systems are often based on stability and performance within existing structures. However, in a change-centric organization, rewards should be tied to innovation, adaptability, and contribution to transformation. Leaders should recognize employees who show initiative, embrace new ways of working, and contribute to the success of the transformation. This reinforces the idea that change is valued and that individuals are rewarded for actively participating in and contributing to the transformation process.

Becoming a Change Catalyst

SCALING YOUR IMPACT AS A DIGITAL LEADER

EMBRACING THE ROLE OF A CATALYST
How to become the spark that ignites change and inspire others to follow

As the pace of change accelerates, the role of the change leader has never been more important. Today, the need for leaders who can catalyze change—inspire transformation, drive innovation, and lead teams through uncertainty—is paramount. But what does it mean to be a change catalyst, and how can you embody this role to influence your organization, team, and even the industry at large? A change catalyst isn't just someone who oversees the change process; they are the driving force that makes transformation happen.

To truly become a catalyst, a leader must first embrace the mindset that change is not something to be managed passively but actively created. The best leaders don't wait for transformation to happen; they actively push the boundaries and encourage others to do the same. They challenge the status quo and ask difficult questions, pushing their teams to rethink processes, reimagine strategies, and embrace new possibilities. By leading from the front, they inspire their team members to take ownership of change and drive it forward, creating a ripple effect that influences the entire organization.

At the heart of this is the ability to inspire and influence others. A change catalyst knows that their role is not just about executing a plan or achieving a goal—they are responsible for motivating and engaging others throughout the journey. They inspire trust and enthusiasm through their actions, words, and personal commitment to the cause. A catalyst's ability to effectively communicate their vision for change is what allows them to rally others around that vision. They make change feel exciting and possible, even when obstacles arise. Their energy is infectious, and they create a sense of momentum that propels the entire organization forward.

To be effective in this role, change catalysts also lead with empathy. They understand that transformation can be challenging and uncomfortable, and they are adept at guiding people through the emotional side of change. By listening to concerns, providing support, and addressing fears, they help ease the transition and reduce resistance. Empathy helps build stronger relationships with employees and teams, and it fosters a safe environment where individuals feel comfortable taking risks, experimenting, and learning. A catalyst's ability to connect with others on an emotional level fosters collaboration, encouraging people to work together toward a common goal.

In addition to empathy, resilience is another key trait of a change catalyst. The journey of transformation is rarely a smooth one. Leaders will face setbacks, challenges, and resistance at almost every stage. What separates successful change catalysts from others is their ability to persevere in the face of adversity. They stay focused on the larger vision, adapting and adjusting their approach as needed. Their resilience encourages others to stay the course, no matter how difficult things may seem. By maintaining a positive, solution-focused attitude, change catalysts help their teams navigate obstacles and stay committed to the change process.

Moreover, being a change catalyst involves empowering others to lead change as well. A true catalyst doesn't just drive change from the top down—they work to build a culture of change throughout the organization. They encourage individuals at all levels to step up, take responsibility, and actively contribute to the transformation. By empowering employees to lead initiatives, take risks, and make decisions, catalysts create a dynamic environment where everyone is invested in the success of the change. This decentralization of leadership allows the organization to scale change more effectively, as it's not reliant on just one or two individuals to keep the momentum going.

Becoming a change catalyst also requires continuous learning. The landscape of business and technology is ever-evolving, and successful change leaders must stay ahead of the curve. A catalyst's ability to adapt and evolve is crucial. They are committed to self-improvement, constantly seeking new knowledge, skills, and perspectives that can enhance their leadership capabilities. Whether through formal education, mentorship, or learning from peers, they understand that growth is a lifelong journey. They encourage their teams to do the same, fostering a culture of learning and development that aligns with the ongoing transformation.

In essence, the role of a change catalyst is one that is proactive, resilient, and collaborative. By taking ownership of the change process, inspiring others, leading with empathy, and remaining adaptable, leaders can become the sparks that ignite transformation across their organizations. They make change feel possible, exciting, and sustainable, ensuring that it becomes an enduring part of the organization's culture and success. As digital leaders, it is the catalyst's role to not only manage transformation but to actively drive it forward, ensuring that their organizations are positioned for long-term growth and innovation.

SPREADING THE CHANGE
How to inspire others to take on the mantle of change leadership

One of the most powerful aspects of being a change catalyst is the ability to spread the desire for transformation throughout the entire organization. As a leader, it is essential to ensure that the vision and values of change are not confined to a select group of leaders or change champions, but are shared by everyone in the organization. A change catalyst doesn't just drive transformation themselves—they inspire others to do the same, creating a culture of continuous improvement where everyone is empowered to lead change in their own capacity.

For leaders who want to foster this kind of organization-wide shift, the first step is to make change everyone's responsibility. It's easy to fall into the trap of delegating transformation to a specific group or department—such as a change management team or a select few senior leaders. However, true transformation only happens when the desire for change is embraced by all employees, regardless of their role. This means that leaders must actively involve employees in the change process, ensuring that they feel like key contributors to the success of the transformation. Employees who feel like they have a personal stake in the change are far more likely to take ownership of it and take proactive steps to contribute.

To spread the change, leaders must create collaborative spaces where employees can come together, share ideas, and collectively brainstorm solutions to challenges. Creating opportunities for employees to connect and collaborate around the transformation encourages innovation and enables cross-functional teams to work together toward a common goal. These spaces could be formal—

such as workshops, brainstorming sessions, and cross-departmental meetings—or informal, like lunch-and-learn events, internal chat channels, or open forums where employees can discuss the transformation and contribute their ideas. By facilitating collaboration, leaders help spread the energy and excitement around change, ensuring that it doesn't just come from the top down but is generated from the ground up.

One of the most effective ways to spread change across the organization is by identifying and empowering change champions at all levels. These are individuals who naturally align with the transformation and who can help drive the change within their teams and departments. Change champions don't have to be senior leaders—they can be anyone who is passionate about the transformation and is willing to lead by example. These champions can be key players in helping spread the change, motivate their colleagues, and influence others to adopt the new behaviors and practices. They act as change ambassadors, encouraging others to embrace the transformation and offering support when challenges arise. Identifying and supporting change champions across the organization allows leaders to multiply their impact and scale transformation more effectively.

Another critical element of spreading change is effective communication. While leaders need to clearly articulate the vision for change, it's equally important that the message resonates at all levels of the organization. Change catalysts need to ensure that communication is frequent, consistent, and inclusive. This means not only sharing information from the top down but also ensuring that employees have the opportunity to provide feedback, ask questions, and express concerns. The more transparent and inclusive the communication process, the more likely employees are to feel engaged and invested in the transformation. It's also important to use multiple channels to communicate the change, ensuring that the message reaches every employee—whether through team meetings, email updates, town halls, or informal discussions. This constant communication helps build a sense of shared purpose, ensuring that everyone is aligned and working toward the same goal.

Recognition and rewards play a significant role in spreading change throughout the organization. When employees take ownership of the transformation and make meaningful contributions to the change process, it's important to acknowledge and celebrate their efforts. Recognition reinforces the desired behaviors and encourages others to follow suit. This can take the form of public recognition in team meetings, rewards for employees who exemplify the values of transformation, or even simple thank-you notes that acknowledge individual efforts. By celebrating the contributions of employees at every level, leaders reinforce the idea that change is everyone's responsibility, and that those who contribute are valued and appreciated.

Leaders must also demonstrate resilience as they spread change across the organization. Transformation is rarely easy, and there will inevitably be challenges, setbacks, and moments of frustration. In these times, it is essential for leaders to model resilience and perseverance. They must continue to communicate the vision and purpose of the change, even when progress seems slow or obstacles arise. When employees see their leaders remain steadfast, even in the face of adversity, it encourages them to stay committed to the process as well. Leaders must encourage their teams to learn from setbacks, view challenges as opportunities for growth, and stay focused on the long-term benefits of the transformation.

SCALING IMPACT BEYOND THE ORGANIZATION
How to expand the influence of change to the wider ecosystem

Change doesn't stop at the organizational boundaries; it radiates outward, influencing partners, customers, and even entire industries. As a change catalyst, your influence can extend beyond the walls of your organization. The transformation you initiate within your company can serve as a model for others, creating ripples that extend into the broader ecosystem. To scale your impact, you must think beyond the organization and embrace your role as a change leader within your industry, network, and community. This means leveraging your company's transformation to influence not only internal stakeholders but also external ones—shaping the future in a broader sense.

One of the first steps in scaling your impact is to collaborate with external partners. In today's interconnected world, transformation rarely happens in isolation. It's essential to build alliances with other organizations, suppliers, and service providers to create a collective impact. Change catalysts should engage with external partners who share similar values and goals, fostering collaboration and mutual support. For example, if your company is transitioning to more sustainable business practices, collaborating with suppliers who prioritize sustainability allows you to scale the change beyond your internal operations. Shared values and aligned goals with partners increase the potential for broad, systemic transformation.

Additionally, engaging with customers is another vital component of scaling impact. Customers are not just passive recipients of products or services; they are active participants in the transformation process. By involving customers in the journey, organizations can create a feedback loop that shapes the product or service offerings and deepens the relationship. In today's world, customers expect companies to innovate, adapt, and deliver value in a way that aligns with their needs and expectations. A change catalyst should ensure that customers are aware of the transformation and that their feedback is incorporated into the process. Customers who feel included in the transformation process become advocates for the organization, spreading the message of change and reinforcing the company's credibility as a leader in its field.

Thought leadership is another powerful way to scale the impact of change. Leaders who serve as catalysts should actively share their knowledge, insights, and experiences with others in their industry. This can be done through speaking engagements, publications, blogs, or social media. By positioning themselves as thought leaders, change catalysts not only expand their influence but also inspire others in their field to adopt similar practices. Through sharing insights on the transformation process—what worked, what didn't, and lessons learned—they can educate others and encourage wider adoption of new practices and ideas. Thought leadership amplifies the impact of a transformation by demonstrating that change is possible, necessary, and effective.

Another strategy to scale the impact of change is by driving industry-wide innovation. Industry leaders who embrace transformation often set the standard for others to follow. As a change catalyst, you should use your organization's success as a springboard to push the boundaries of industry innovation. Whether it's through the introduction of new technologies, methodologies, or business models, your efforts can influence how the broader market adapts to change. Leaders who champion industry innovation help shift the paradigm, inspiring others to pursue similar initiatives and making systemic change more likely. For example, if your organization is a pioneer in digitizing customer service, your success can inspire others in the industry to follow suit, leading to a widespread shift toward digitally-enabled services.

Furthermore, change catalysts can influence the larger ecosystem by advocating for policy changes. As organizations undergo transformation, they often encounter regulatory and policy barriers that slow progress. Advocating for change at the policy level allows leaders to address these external challenges and influence the broader landscape. Change catalysts can engage in discussions with industry associations, policymakers, or government bodies to ensure that the rules, regulations, and standards keep pace with the transformation happening within organizations. By actively contributing to policy discussions, you help create an environment that supports continued innovation and change. This advocacy not only drives systemic change but also positions your organization as a leader in shaping the future of the industry.

Leaders can also leverage community involvement to scale their impact. By engaging with local communities, non-profits, and social enterprises, organizations can extend their transformation efforts into the social sphere, addressing issues that go beyond business objectives. For example, if your company is focusing on sustainability, partnering with environmental organizations or supporting community sustainability programs creates a broader social impact. Engaging with local communities can help align the company's goals with societal needs, ensuring that the transformation benefits not just the business but also the people and environment it impacts. Community involvement strengthens the company's reputation as a responsible, ethical organization that is committed to positive change on multiple levels.

In addition to community engagement, networking plays a pivotal role in scaling impact. Building a network of like-minded individuals—whether through professional organizations, industry events, or informal groups—can amplify your efforts and provide support when navigating challenges. A strong network allows change catalysts to share insights, collaborate on projects, and leverage collective resources. By engaging with other leaders who are also committed to transformation, you can create a powerful coalition that drives change together, making a bigger impact than any one organization or leader could achieve alone. Networking also provides access to new ideas, enabling leaders to continually evolve their transformation efforts.

CREATING A LEGACY OF CHANGE
How to ensure that the changes you initiate continue to shape the future

As a change catalyst, your role extends far beyond executing a transformation successfully—it's about creating a legacy of change that persists long after the transformation is completed. The ability to establish lasting change is what distinguishes short-term wins from meaningful, long-term success. A true change catalyst does not just lead a project; they build the foundations for continuous innovation, growth, and transformation within the organization. They ensure that the impact of their leadership extends into the future, affecting both the organization and the wider community in profound and enduring ways.

The first step in creating a legacy of change is to institutionalize the transformation. For change to become permanent, it must be woven into the organization's very fabric. This means ensuring that the changes made during the transformation are integrated into the organization's values, practices, and structures. This could involve incorporating new practices into standard operating procedures, aligning systems and technologies with the new way of working, and ensuring that the leadership pipeline is built around the skills and values that support the transformation. By embedding the change into the fabric of the organization, it becomes a core component of the organizational identity, something that will continue to shape the company long after the initial transformation.

Equally important is developing the next generation of leaders. One of the key ways to create a lasting legacy is by ensuring that the leaders of tomorrow are equipped with the knowledge, skills, and mindset needed to continue driving change. Change catalysts should focus on leadership development as part of their transformation efforts. This involves mentoring and empowering emerging leaders, encouraging them to take on responsibility for future initiatives, and providing them with the tools and experiences they need to become change agents in their own right. When you invest in leadership development, you are ensuring that the values and principles of the transformation continue to thrive and evolve long after the current leaders have moved on.

Creating a legacy of change also involves ensuring that learning is continuous. Change catalysts understand that the world is constantly evolving, and therefore, so must the organization. To create a sustainable legacy, it's essential that the organization remains committed to learning and growth. This means establishing systems for ongoing development, such as training programs, knowledge-sharing platforms, and learning networks. When organizations prioritize learning, they create an environment where new ideas and innovations can thrive, ensuring that change is not a one-time event but a continuous process. Leaders should promote curiosity, encourage employees to ask questions, and allow them to explore new ideas and approaches that will help the organization stay ahead of the curve.

To fostering a learning culture, recognition and reward systems should be aligned with the new values and behaviors introduced during the transformation. By reinforcing the desired behaviors through regular recognition, leaders can ensure that these behaviors are sustained over time. Incentives, whether financial or non-financial, should reward those who embody the new ways of working and contribute to the ongoing transformation. Publicly celebrating individuals and teams who embrace change fosters an atmosphere where innovation and growth are valued and where people are motivated to continue driving transformation. This recognition helps embed the transformation into the corporate culture, ensuring that it remains a long-lasting part of the company's ethos.

Another important aspect of creating a legacy of change is building strong relationships and partnerships with external stakeholders. Change catalysts recognize that their impact doesn't stop at the company's borders. By fostering strong relationships with customers, suppliers, community leaders, and even competitors, they can help ensure that the change has wider resonance and that the benefits of transformation extend beyond the organization. These partnerships can help drive industry-wide change, create opportunities for collaboration, and amplify the impact of the transformation in meaningful ways. Strong relationships also help safeguard the sustainability of the changes, as external stakeholders can act as additional advocates for the changes within the organization.

Building a legacy of change requires leaders to be focused on the long term. A short-term mindset can undermine the sustainability of the transformation, leading to quick fixes rather than lasting solutions. Leaders must always keep the long-term vision in mind, understanding that true transformation is a gradual process that requires patience and dedication. They should plan for the future, ensuring that the changes they are implementing today will continue to shape the organization's direction and impact years down the line. This means not only setting short-term goals but also thinking ahead about how the transformation can be scaled and adapted as the organization grows.

LEADING CHANGE WITH PURPOSE
How to ensure your leadership is aligned with both organizational goals and a higher purpose

Leadership during times of transformation demands more than just strategic thinking and operational efficiency. It requires a deep sense of purpose—a guiding principle that aligns both the organization's goals and the broader impact it wants to have in the world. A leader who can tie their transformation efforts to a clear higher purpose creates a powerful, motivating force that transcends tactical objectives. By embedding purpose into every aspect of the transformation process, change catalysts can inspire not only their teams but the entire organization to commit to long-term success.

One of the first steps in leading change with purpose is to clearly define the organization's purpose. For a leader, this means understanding not only the practical goals of the transformation but also the deeper, long-term impact the organization seeks to create. This could be a commitment to sustainability, improving customer experiences, advancing diversity and inclusion, or contributing to broader societal progress. Leaders who can articulate a clear, compelling vision of purpose create a shared sense of mission that inspires employees at every level of the organization. When employees understand that their work contributes to a larger, meaningful goal, they are more motivated, engaged, and aligned with the transformation.

Leaders must also model purpose-driven behavior. It is not enough to simply talk about the purpose; leaders must demonstrate it through their actions and decisions. Purpose-driven leaders consistently prioritize what matters most, even when faced with difficult decisions or pressures to pursue short-term gains. Whether it's choosing to make an investment in sustainability initiatives, offering additional support to employees during difficult transitions, or taking a stand on social or ethical issues, purpose-driven leaders make decisions that are aligned with their organization's values. When leaders consistently model purpose, they set the tone for the entire organization, creating a culture where purpose is a priority, not just a talking point.

Purpose-driven leadership also requires leaders to empower employees to connect their work to the organization's higher purpose. It's not enough to just have a purpose statement; employees must be able to see how their individual contributions are aligned with that purpose. Leaders can facilitate this connection by helping employees understand the larger mission and how their role supports it. Whether through team meetings, one-on-one discussions, or company-wide communications, leaders should regularly remind employees of the broader impact of their work. By fostering a culture of purpose-driven work, leaders ensure that employees feel that their contributions are not just valued, but also aligned with something greater than themselves.

Another essential element of leading change with purpose is to ensure that all decisions are made through the lens of purpose. Every choice—whether it's about resource allocation, technology investments, or partnerships—should be viewed through the filter of the organization's core mission. For example, if an organization's purpose is to be environmentally sustainable, then decision-making processes must prioritize sustainability goals. Leaders who integrate purpose into every decision help ensure that transformation efforts are not just tactical but are aligned with the long-term vision for the organization. Purpose-driven decision-making helps steer the organization through challenges, ensuring that the direction remains true, even when faced with obstacles or competing priorities.

In addition to making decisions that reflect the organization's values, leaders must communicate the purpose of the transformation at every stage. Transformational change can be complex and overwhelming, and it's easy for employees to become focused on the tactical elements rather than the overarching mission. By consistently reiterating the connection between the transformation and the organization's core purpose, leaders can help teams stay focused on the broader vision. Communication should focus on why the change is important, how it aligns with the organization's values, and the lasting impact it will have on employees, customers, and the community at large. Purpose-driven communication helps employees see the big picture, making it easier for them to remain engaged and motivated throughout the transformation.

Leaders should also create opportunities for reflection throughout the transformation process. Reflection allows individuals and teams to reconnect with the purpose of the change and evaluate whether their actions are aligned with the organization's mission. Whether through formal mechanisms such as surveys or feedback sessions, or more informal conversations, reflection provides employees with the space to re-evaluate their role in the transformation and re-affirm their commitment to the organization's values. Reflection also creates a sense of ownership and personal accountability. When employees reflect on their contributions, they feel more engaged and motivated to continue their work.

Recognizing and celebrating purpose-driven achievements reinforces the connection between the transformation and the organization's values. Leaders should acknowledge and celebrate both individual and team efforts that demonstrate alignment with the organization's purpose. Recognition can take many forms, from public shout-outs during meetings to formal awards or incentives. Celebrating purpose-driven achievements helps solidify the connection between employees' everyday work and the larger mission, reinforcing the idea that the change is meaningful, impactful, and worth pursuing.

Bibliography

- Cagan, Marty. *Inspired: How to Create Tech Products Customers Love*. Wiley, 2018.
- Ries, Eric. *The Lean Startup: How Today's Entrepreneurs Use Continuous Innovation to Create Radically Successful Businesses*. Crown Business, 2011.
- Kotter, John P. *Leading Change*. Harvard Business Review Press, 2012.
- Westerman, George; Bonnet, Didier; McAfee, Andrew. *Leading Digital: Turning Technology into Business Transformation*. Harvard Business Review Press, 2014.
- Brynjolfsson, Erik; McAfee, Andrew. *The Second Machine Age: Work, Progress, and Prosperity in a Time of Brilliant Technologies*. W.W. Norton & Company, 2014.
- Davenport, Thomas H.; Ronanki, Rajeev. *Artificial Intelligence for the Real World*. Harvard Business Review, 2018.
- Brown, Tim. *Change by Design: How Design Thinking Creates New Alternatives for Business and Society*. Harvard Business Review Press, 2009.
- Goleman, Daniel. *Emotional Intelligence: Why It Can Matter More Than IQ*. Bantam, 2006.
- Laloux, Frederic. *Reinventing Organizations: A Guide to Creating Organizations Inspired by the Next Stage of Human Consciousness*. Nelson Parker, 2014.
- Sinek, Simon. *Start with Why: How Great Leaders Inspire Everyone to Take Action*. Portfolio, 2009.
- Schwab, Klaus. *The Fourth Industrial Revolution*. World Economic Forum, 2017.
- World Economic Forum. *The Future of Jobs Report*. 2023. www.weforum.org
- McKinsey & Company. *The State of AI in 2023*. www.mckinsey.com
- Gartner. *Top Strategic Technology Trends*. 2023. www.gartner.com

Printed in Great Britain
by Amazon